TARNISHED EXPANSION

TARNISHED EXPANSION
The Alaska Scandal, the Press, and Congress, 1867–1871

PAUL S. HOLBO

The University of Tennessee Press / Knoxville

FIRST EDITION.

FRONTISPIECE: The Alaska Treaty by Emanuel Leutze. Reproduced from *Seward at Washington* (1891).

CLOTHBOUND EDITIONS OF UNIVERSITY OF TENNESSEE PRESS BOOKS ARE PRINTED ON PAPER DESIGNED FOR AN EFFECTIVE LIFE OF AT LEAST 300 YEARS, AND BINDING MATERIALS ARE CHOSEN FOR STRENGTH AND DURABILITY.

LIBRARY OF CONGRESS CATALOGING IN PUBLICATION DATA

Holbo, Paul Sothe.
  Tarnished expansion.
  Bibliography: p.
  Includes index.
  1. United States—Politics and government—1865–1877.
2. United States—Foreign relations—1865–1898. 3. Alaska—History—1867–1896. 4. United States—Territorial expansion.
5. Corruption (in politics)—United States—History—19th century. 6. Press and politics—United States. I. Title.
E669.H64 1983   973.8   82-17513
ISBN 0-87049-380-9

TO MY PARENTS
John and Dagny Sothe Holbo
WHO TAUGHT ME TO AVOID SCANDAL

ACKNOWLEDGMENTS

I am grateful to a number of persons for their assistance in the research that resulted in this book and in a continuing larger project of which this is a part. I appreciate especially the help provided by Scott Carlin of Greenbelt, Maryland, a former undergraduate student who took time from his dissertation work to aid in checking evidence. Lewis L. Gould of the University of Texas, John Niven of the Claremont Graduate School, and Margaret Thompson Echols, then a graduate student at the University of Wisconsin, made valuable suggestions at key moments in my work. Richard Brown of the Newberry Library, whose helpfulness to visitors is unsurpassed, provided necessary facilities and advice.

I also thank the staffs of a number of other institutions for providing materials and responding to my entreaties. These include the Manuscripts Division and the Newspaper Room of the Library of Congress, the National Archives, the Manuscripts Room of the New York Public Library, the Essex Institute, the Newberry Library, the Historical Society of Pennsylvania, the Manuscripts and Special Collections Division of the New York State Library (especially Christine M. Missoff), the University of Oregon Library, the P.K. Yonge Library of Florida History of the University of Florida, the Florida State Archives (especially Richard Roberts), the Florida Historical Society (especially Paul Eugen Camp), and the Kansas Historical Society.

I am indebted as well to Mavis Bryant of the University of Tennessee Press for her interest in my work and her continuing encouragement, to Katherine Holloway for her suggestions, and to other thoughtful reviewers for that press.

The Kansas State Historical Society provided valuable photographs and generously authorized their use. Photographer Harry Houchins ably and inexpensively reproduced a number of pictures from the University of Oregon's collections. The other illustrations were obtained from the Matthew Brady and general collections of the Prints and Photographs Reading Room of the Library of Congress, and were reproduced by that Library's expensive but expert Photoduplication Service. I regret that I was unable to find a photograph of newspaper correspondent Uriah Painter, despite extensive searches and the best efforts of the staffs of several libraries and historical societies. Investigative reporters were not so famous in that day as in our own, but, as will be seen, they were fully as important.

PAUL S. HOLBO
Eugene, Oregon
August 9, 1982

CONTENTS

ILLUSTRATIONS

INTRODUCTION

Corruption is the sordid underside of public life. The American people, abetted by the press and by politicians themselves, believe in their more cynical moments that corruption goes hand-in-pocket with government. Blanket condemnation is unfair, for there are many honest officeholders, but several generations of Americans have had considerable justification for holding jaundiced views about those who govern. One needs only to recall Teapot Dome and the Truman scandals as well as recent familiar misconduct such as Watergate, Koreagate, and Abscam.

Sensational revelations of recent vintage sometimes obscure the embarrassing fact that dishonesty in government, frequently accompanied by suspicions of corruption, has occurred throughout American history. Well before the first shots were fired at Lexington Green, American smugglers eluded or bribed thieving English admiralty officers. The Revolution finally took place, it has been argued, when Americans concluded that the British government headed by King George III was hopelessly degraded.[1]

Fortunately, schoolchildren are not required to memorize the list of scandals in American government that followed the Revolution — as they are, all too often, compelled to recite the names of Presidents and battles, or remember the virtues of remarkable women, Blacks, and reformers — for the chronicle of corruption is lengthy. Not only is the raw material plentiful, the scandalous episodes are often very complicated. Most teachers, perhaps rightly, emphasize more elevated events, unless they are sermonizing upon the sins of a party or administration that they particularly detest.

On the whole, scandal and the suspicion of corruption are neglected subjects in American history. This is unfortunate because these topics are of inherent interest to scholars, students, and citizens generally, and because some of the lowpoints in American public morality have been of considerable political importance. There are, of course, exceptions to this rule. Historians have debated at length the extent of speculation in public lands and public securities by the fathers of the Constitution. Without a doubt, speculation did occur, but its significance for the drafting and adoption of that document remains in doubt.[2]

The Yazoo land frauds of the 1790s provide a clearer case in both fact and consequence. This tangled affair involved the sale at 1.5 cents an acre of 35 million acres of public lands. Every member but one of the Georgia legislature was interested in a company designed to profit enormously from the transaction. Subsequent revelations and attempts to undo the sales led to legal battles which reached the Supreme Court (*Fletcher* v. *Peck*, 1810). These events and the efforts of the Jefferson administration to reach a compromise with Congress in the complex case shaped the attitudes of influential Republicans toward James Madison and other principals for more than a decade.[3]

One further example from the history of the early republic may make the point that, even in those simpler days, corruption was astonishing in extent, occurred repeatedly, and had political effects. Before the odor of the unsavory Yazoo episode had entirely faded, the Jacksonian "spoils system" tarnished and impoverished government. More was involved than merely a turnover in officeholders and opportunities for appointments from the "mob" of common people. The man whom President Andrew Jackson named customs collector of the Port of New York, Samuel Swartwout, embezzled $1,226,000 during his two terms in office. Jackson's successor, Martin Van Buren, who had opposed Swartwout's appointment, filled the place with Jesse Hoyt, who was more thoroughly dishonest than his predecessor, although he managed to steal a comparatively modest $350,000. Such were the benefits of the Jacksonian practice of "rotation in office." It was, as historian Edward Pessen has observed, a materialistic as well as democratic era.[4] Some Americans reacted by becoming Whigs and supporting appointments to office for merit.

There have been many similar episodes. The pages that follow will briefly mention several of the scandals of the era following the Civil War, including the whisky frauds, in which crooked federal revenue agents bilked the treasury of excise taxes due from distillers; the Fernando Wood machine in New York City, which set the pattern for the Tweed Ring and Tammany Hall; and Credit Mobilier, the company which built the government-subsidized Union Pacific Railroad and bought congressmen to prevent disclosure of its excessive profits. This recital does not imply that there was more dishonesty in the Gilded Age than in other periods; the extent of corruption in the Gilded Age has often been exaggerated, as historian Ari Hoogenboom has observed.[5] But the scandals that did occur and some unwarranted suspicions aroused reformers, inspired editorials, and affected presidential campaigns and local politics. Voters reacted to these events, too, as they did to the revelations after 1950 about gifts of "mink coats and deep freezers" to members of the Truman administration and after 1972 to the Watergate scandal.

Scholarly writing on scandal in American political history is sparse. There was much muckraking literature early in the twentieth century, notably such exposés of municipal corruption as Lincoln Steffens's *The Shame of the Cities* (1904). Many later scholarly histories and biographies, especially those dealing with reform movements and with urban life, treated corruption in passing. Prior to Watergate, however, there was only one historical article devoted to the general subject of corruption, and that brief piece focused once again on the character of urban political machines.[6]

During the Watergate investigation, the House Judiciary Committee commissioned the publication of a "factual and non-interpretive" study of the responses of presidents to charges of misconduct. A judicious volume resulted, but the studies of individual presidents are necessarily brief.[7] Morton Keller's monumental analysis of public affairs in late nineteenth-century America contains thoughtful reflections on corruption, as does his chapter in the fine book resulting from a symposium at Brooklyn College on corruption "before Watergate."[8] There is also an important recent multivolume set of essays and documents on selected congressional investigations.[9] There are, in addition, capable analyses of selected episodes such as the Star Route cases, the St. Louis Whisky Ring, and Teapot Dome.[10] Watergate, of course, spawned a virtual deluge of publications and lectures about that scandal and its disclosure.

This monograph extends the brief list of studies of earlier scandals by looking at the Alaska scandal and investigations during 1868 and 1869. The Alaska affair is of particular interest because it involved foreign as well as domestic concerns, as have several scandals in more recent times. It has been investigated extensively by careful scholars over a period of seventy years.[11] The political context — pervasive suspicions of corruption — has never been described, however, and new evidence on specific allegations about Alaska continues to emerge.

The search for documents is, of course, one of the special delights and the peculiar frustration of studying corruption. Evidence of good deeds comes to light easily, but corruption is by nature hidden activity and is often obscured by careful attempts to forestall disclosure. Dishonesty in public affairs is usually revealed, if at all, by government investigation. It must be recognized that, in American politics, investigation often follows upon the heels of corruption. Corruption recurs irrepressibly, but, when it becomes too apparent, Americans usually seem determined to expose it, obliterate it, or put it behind them. Public investigations have their limitations, however, as will be seen in this study, and not everything is disclosed owing to political and other interests. Hence, historians enjoy the opportunity to search for further materials and to explain any remaining mysteries.

All good history involves the uncovering and explanation of the previously unknown, but the historian of corruption inherently faces more problems in exposing who did it and how the crimes were managed. It must be admitted that historians cannot explain every element of the plot, for they are unlike writers of fictional mysteries who have invented the crucial details of their stories. In history, some elements remain unclear because the facts are not yet known or are in dispute and perhaps can never be known. Historians must search for evidence as best they can, but it is not necessary for them to bring out every conceivable detail. Their fundamental task is to address larger issues.

This book grew out of an effort to answer one such important question: Was the United States an imperialist nation in the late nineteenth century? As my study progressed, it became clear that scandal and suspicion of corruption had marred the course of expansionism in the Gilded Age. My resulting inquiry into the relation between expansionism and scandal has encompassed five episodes: Alaska, Santo Domingo, Samoa, Hawaii, and Cuba. Analysis of the Alaska scandal, which I had assumed was well understood, quickly revealed that much about it needed retelling. Significant features of this story demanded substantial evidence to be convincing and required more space than I could provide in my continuing larger study, in which I must limit details because of the number of episodes and the need to develop broad patterns. Hence I have written this separate, brief volume on the Alaska scandal.

A study of the Alaska affair is in order because of the subject's inherent fascination, its importance, and its larger implications. The purchase of Alaska was, of course, one of this nation's greatest real estate transactions. The story of this deal needs to be explored as fully as possible.

I have discovered some new material about the Alaska scandal and analyzed the affair afresh. As a result of this historical detective work, I can with considerable certainty identify several of the villains in the piece. Of greater importance is the fact that this study describes for the first time the development of the original investigations of the scandal by the press and by Congress, and notes the ironic turns that these inquiries took.

There have been similar events in recent times, and the patterns merit reflection. The larger point is that the reaction to the Alaska scandal was even more important than the wrongdoing itself. We have for some years known that editors, politicians, and other Americans had somewhat mixed responses to the *purchase* of Alaska. Their reaction to the *scandal* has been overlooked but was more significant than the debate over "Seward's folly," for the revelations in the press and the congressional investigation had an enduring effect on the course of American foreign policy.

The significance of this thesis must be made explicit, lest it be overlooked. Americans in the nineteenth and early twentieth centuries possessed definite feelings on the issue of territorial expansion. Some politicians and publicists defended and others attacked the idea, but the question of expansion was very real for them. This perspective changed as the years passed. One reason is that expansionism did not come to much. After the acquisition of Alaska in 1867, the United States added nothing to its domain prior to the war against Spain. After a brief flurry at the end of the century, expansion quickly ceased again. There was only limited expansion, scholars suggested, because the United States presumably was weary from the Civil War or preoccupied with the tasks of settling the west and of urban and industrial development.[12]

Historians and others writing during and after the Second World War on the subject of American foreign relations in their own or in earlier times particularly de-emphasized the expansionism of the United States.[13] They no doubt were influenced by the life-and-death struggle waged against Nazi and fascist expansionism and by the new emphasis under the United Nations of respect for one's neighbors. The minimizing of American territorial aims in the late nineteenth century became the prevailing view in historical interpretation. Curiously, it influenced even those writers, labeled revisionists, who in the 1960s severely criticized United States foreign policy. The revisionists did not generally accuse the United States of territorial expansionism, perhaps because there was so little evidence of acquisitions. Instead, the revisionists contended that the United States had sought commercial expansion throughout its history and in the late nineteenth century had pursued an open door for markets abroad instead of territory overseas.[14]

Both the prevailing and the revisionist interpretations are incorrect, in my view. There was, in fact, substantial territorial expansionism, especially after the Civil War and at the very time when the United States was supposedly preoccupied by internal events. After 1865 the newly powerful though financially straitened national government simultaneously pursued both reconstruction of the south and territorial expansion. Indeed, while President Andrew Johnson and Representative Thaddeus Stevens—to mention just two leading figures—disagreed bitterly about reconstruction, they were of one mind about expansion. The expansionism continued throughout the decade after the war, moreover, and surfaced again in the early 1890s.

The postwar period was one of large policy goals at the national level, but it also was a time of contrary, divisive tendencies: sensational journalism, easily aroused suspicions of corrupt and selfish interests, political opportunism, partisanship, and personal hatreds. These disruptive if quite democratic factors—which recur frequently in American public life—helped to make reconstruction a bloody political battlefield, and they blunted the expansionism of the Gilded Age. In the case of expansionism, the scandals and the allegations of corruption were of particular importance. Beginning with the Alaska scandal, the charges of dishonesty and the suspicions that erupted during each expansionist episode were the crucial factors in frustrating the efforts of those who wanted to extend the American domain.

Alaska, therefore, was not merely the last territorial acquisition for more than thirty years; it was the issue of corruption in the appropriation for Alaska that tarnished the expansionists' efforts and placed substantial roadblocks in their path. To put it another way, the purchase of Alaska, which expansionists had seen as one of the first fruits of their labors, proved to be their final success because of the scandal that ensued.

TARNISHED EXPANSION

CHAPTER ONE

THE ACQUISITION OF ALASKA
The Setting for the "Crime" and the Characters in the Plot

The story of "Seward's folly" is a well-worn schoolbook tale. Almost every American knows that the United States purchased Alaska at a bargain price and that the territory, now highly valued for its strategic location and resources, once was dubbed a worthless "ice box" and region of "perpetual icebergs."

Historians have explored extensively the records of this seemingly simple real estate deal. Diligent scholars have described forerunners to the sale and carefully pieced together analyses of Russia's motives for disposing of the territory, the brief diplomatic negotiations, and the generally favorable responses of American editors and "public opinion."[1] There are even several judicious accounts of the seamy underside of the transaction — the alleged bribery of American journalists and congressmen by the Russian minister to the United States, Edouard de Stoeckl, to secure passage of the appropriation of $7,200,000 by the House of Representatives.[2]

These admirable narratives ordinarily would not need to be related again. Nor is it important to revise them merely for the sake of correcting occasional errors or adding details. A review of the acquisition of Alaska is essential, however, for understanding the frustration of American expansionism between 1867 and 1898. Paradoxically, the aftermath of Secretary of State William H. Seward's hard-won success with Alaska jeopardized later ventures, notably the repeated efforts by President Ulysses S. Grant to annex the Dominican Republic. Altogether, the Alaska affair helped to fix patterns of politics that characterized much of the Gilded Age, and it illuminates the larger record of United States foreign policy as well as important recurring peculiarities of American public behavior. This is the story of the rise and the ebb of American policy and activism — the pursuit of large goals, vitiated by sensational charges, revelations of scandal, suspicions, and opportunistic politics.

In December 1868, the United States House of Representatives opened hearings into the "Alaska Scandal." These were set off by newspaper stories earlier that year of Russian payments to congressmen and journalists to secure an appropriation of $7,200,000 for the purchase of Alaska. One of the prominent witnesses before the Committee on Public Expenditures was Robert J. Walker, former senator from Mississippi, political architect of the election of 1844, secretary of the Treasury under President James K. Polk, governor of Kansas Territory, and financial agent in Europe for President Abraham Lincoln.

The inquiry brought out that Walker — still active as a Democratic politician and among the leading Washington lawyers of the day — had served as "counsel" to the Russian minister during the Alaska affair. Governor Walker defended himself aggressively by telling the committee that he was not simply a paid advocate of the purchase of Alaska but had repeatedly recommended its acquisition over many years. He asserted that more than two decades earlier, on March 3, 1845, he had responded to Polk's request that he become secretary of the Treasury by urging the President-elect to obtain the "whole of Oregon" and predicting that a friendly Russia would "then cede to us her North American territory."[3]

Walker's original Alaskan expectations withered upon the demise of "fifty-four forty," which would have absorbed much of British Columbia into Oregon. But a small circle of like-minded Democrats devised similar projects as the years passed. In 1854, Senator William M. Gwin of California, an old crony of Walker and exponent of the need for foreign territories and trade, served as a go-between for Stoeckl and the administration of Franklin Pierce. The occasion was a far-fetched scheme of the Russian-American Company, a chartered Russian monopoly of the fur trade and other enterprises, to arrange a fictitious sale of the territory to a San Francisco firm in order to protect it from England during the Crimean War. Gwin and Secretary of State William L. Marcy rejected the ruse as transparent, hence impractical; but the senator confided to Stoeckl that the United States would agree to purchase Russian America. The envoy responded at that time that the territory was not for sale. Gwin ventured the proposition again in 1859, with the approval of President James Buchanan. The senator suggested a price of $5 million to Stoeckl, who forwarded his own favorable recommendation to St. Petersburg.[4]

Walker revived the idea in 1863, during a trip abroad to raise funds for the Union in the European financial markets. His traveling companion was another expansionist Democrat, Minister to Russia Cassius M. Clay. On their Atlantic voyage and later in St. Petersburg, Walker told Clay that opportunities to obtain Russian America had been missed during the Polk and Buchanan administrations. The flamboyant Clay declared that the United States should secure the entire west coast of North America. Some months later, on November 14, 1864, Clay wrote to Secretary Seward that it soon would be to the interest of the United States to purchase the territory.[5]

Seward was eager for the chance. An inveterate Republican expansionist and advocate of increased trade, especially with Asia, he believed that America's "gracious destiny" was to create a free, progressive, enlightened, moral empire, which would be a model for the world. He had argued as early as 1846 that the United States should stretch "to the icy barriers of the north." The wartime depredations of the Confederate commerce destroyer *Shenandoah* in the North Pacific convinced him that the United States needed a naval outpost in that region, according to his son and assistant, Frederick Seward.[6] The secretary, a practiced politician at appealing to public opinion, also sensed that such an acquisition would redound to his own credit and benefit the administration in its postwar relations with Congress.

Russia all the while was moving at a glacial pace toward withdrawal from North America. On the eve of the Crimean War, in 1853, some fearful shareholders of the Russian-American Company had urged that the territory be sold to the United States before it was lost to England. An extraordinary neutrality arrangement instead was worked out with the Hudson's Bay Company, but the fact that Russian America survived only by England's sufferance rankled Stoeckl and other Russian officials. Following the war, the government badly needed money. Grand Duke Constantine, who was the emperor's brother and head of the admiralty, which was responsible for administering Russian America, repeatedly contended that the territory should be sold because it could not be defended in any future naval war and would eventually be the goal of American annexationists.[7] He reminded hesitant Prince Gorchakov, the foreign minister, of "the straitened circumstances of the State finances" when he wrote in the spring of 1857 that "we would do well to take advantage of the excess of money at the present time in the Treasury of the United States of America and to sell them our North American colonies." Russia, moreover, had turned its attention in the Far East toward the Amur River.[8]

Stoeckl, sensing that monopoly companies were doomed, strongly supported Constantine. The "Baron," as Americans often referred to him although he did not actually possess a title, had been stationed in the United States since 1841 and was married to a native of Springfield, Massachusetts. Having observed the ways of American democracy, he recommended withdrawing gracefully from Russian America in advance of what he believed was the inevitable expansion of the United States. Late in 1857 Stoeckl reported that he had asked President James Buchanan whether rumored Mormon emigrants to Russian America would come as conquerors or colonists. Buchanan, reflecting current prejudices against the Mormons, had replied with a laugh that it was up to Russia but that he would be very happy to be "rid of them." Stoeckl conceded in his despatch that the Mormons posed no immediate danger but again urged sale of the territory to avoid trouble with the United States. Alexander II penned on the margin of the minister's report: "This supports the idea of a regulation forthwith on the question of our American possessions." Gorchakov at this time directed Stoeckl that an American offer could be considered discreetly.[9]

Following Senator Gwin's overture in 1859, Stoeckl told Gorchakov that the proposal was opportune because of the decreasing profitability of the fur trade, the colony's isolation, and its defenselessness. The sale also would be a blow against England. The foreign minister did not favor cession but instructed his envoy to seek more than the $5 million suggested by Gwin and insisted that the United States take the initiative. He consented meanwhile to Constantine's request for a commission of inquiry to Russian America. The commission's report and a special imperial review committee recommended reform of the territory. By that time sectional conflict in the United States made a cession impossible.[10]

Throughout the period of the American Civil War, the Russian-American Company verged on collapse. Coal mining, ice, and lumber operations failed, while the fur trade declined. Even with a substantial government subsidy, dividends in 1866 were less than 1.5 percent, while shares once valued at 500 rubles fell as low as 75 on the stock market. Reports of gold discoveries after 1860 raised fears in the Russian government that hordes of American miners would overrun the territory, and the company first stifled disclosures, then tried to belittle the findings in order to protect what remained of its interests.[11]

Good political relations between the two nations after 1861, aided by recognition of mutual differences with England and France, helped to keep alive the possibility of selling the territory. Informed Americans were aware that the Russian fleet visited the United States during wartime for strategic reasons, not as a gesture of support for the Union. But Seward and other officials entertained the Russian visitors warmly, and the adept secretary later invited Grand Duke Constantine to come to this country.[12]

After the war, Constantine learned from Stoeckl that the United States might still purchase Russian America. He and other officials pressed the cession for economic and military reasons. Foreign Minister Gorchakov at last agreed because he wished to preserve good relations with the United States, wanted to thwart Great Britain, and feared inevitable American expansion. In a meeting of December 1866, the emperor, Constantine, Gorchakov, and the ministers of finance and marine decided to cede the territory. They directed Stoeckl, who attended the meeting, to transact the deal. His orders were that the United States must initiate the negotiations, so as to preserve Russia's dignity, and pay not less than $5 million.[13]

Stoeckl stopped briefly in New York to recover from a sprained ankle incurred on his voyage. From his hotel room he dispatched Robert J. Walker — or possibly it was Thurlow Weed, veteran lobbyist, friend, and adviser to Seward, and soon to be publisher of the New York *Commercial Advertiser* — to remind the secretary of Russian America's value.[14] Back in Washington by March 1867, Stoeckl cagily informed Seward that his government could not permit a San Francisco firm to lease some of the Hudson's Bay Company's operations in the territory; this was a venture that Minister Clay and Senator Cornelius Cole of California favored. He likewise rejected a plea from the secretary on behalf of citizens of Washington Territory, whose legislature had petitioned the federal government to seek fishing rights off the coasts of Russian America. Seward then inquired if Russia would sell her colony. Stoeckl took this vague overture to satisfy Gorchakov's demand that the United States request the purchase. Negotiations ensued after Seward obtained President Johnson's consent.[15]

At the outset Seward rebuffed the envoy's suggestion that the measure originate with Stoeckl's friends on Capitol Hill. The secretary insisted that it was his responsibility and must be kept secret from Congress until the negotiation was completed. He informally bid $5 million for the territory but suggested incautiously that the offer might go to $5.5 million, though not more. The grasping Stoeckl said nothing but wired his government that he would try for $6.5 million or at least for $6 million. Only a few persons knew of these preliminary negotiations until March 15, when the secretary revealed his draft agreement at a meeting of the cabinet and proposed to pay up to $7 million. His colleagues unanimously agreed, while President Johnson listened but said nothing. Four days later the full cabinet approved a version revised to meet previous criticisms.

Seward resumed haggling with Stoeckl, who now asked for $7 million. The secretary, concerned about the approaching adjournment of Congress and anxious to close the deal, eagerly escalated his offer to the full $7 million. Stoeckl barely disguised his satisfaction. After the emperor authorized him to sign, Stoeckl belatedly raised the issues of prompt payment and compensation for private Russian interests in the territory. Seward explained that payment depended upon a congressional appropriation, which was assured by the honor of the United States. He also demanded that the cession "be free and unincumbered by any reservations, privileges, franchises, grants or possessions by any associated companies." In the end he appeased Stoeckl with an additional $200,000, which the envoy quickly accepted.[16]

On the evening of March 29, Stoeckl appeared at Seward's home to inform him that his government had wired approval of the treaty and that he would come to the Department of State the next day to conclude the transaction. Frederick Seward wrote later that his father rose from a game of whist and suggested, "Why wait till tomorrow, Mr. Stoeckl? Let us make the treaty to-night." Assistants were summoned, and Seward hurried to his office a mile away while Charles Sumner of Massachusetts, the chairman of the Senate Foreign Relations Committee, was called to the Seward home. Young Seward and Stoeckl, who knew the senator well, explained the treaty to him and asked that he support it the next day when the document reached the Senate. Sumner listened without comment. Stoeckl pleaded with the senator as he departed around midnight, "You will not fail us." Sumner, more circumspect than he was to be on a similar occasion three years later, when he caused President Ulysses S. Grant to think that he would support a Dominican annexation treaty, carefully made no promise. Stoeckl and Frederick Seward then joined the secretary at the Department of State. By 4 A.M., March 30, the treaty was perfected.[17]

The events of that long night are fixed in popular history by frequent retelling of Frederick Seward's account and by artist Emanuel Leutze's imaginative painting of the signing.[18] (The secretary's admirers commissioned Leutze's group portrait and presented it to him as a gift for his home; Seward, as will appear, often proudly showed the handsome painting to guests and talked about the treaty's passage.) Seward's numerous detractors, in contrast, described his handiwork as a "deed done in the dark of the night." This was an unfair charge, as the negotiations already had been effectively concluded, with only minor issues to be resolved and sufficient copies made.

The secretary rushed this work to completion because he mistakenly hoped that the Senate would ratify the treaty before Congress adjourned at noon the next day. President Johnson and members of his Cabinet went to Capitol Hill with the treaty at 10 A.M. on Saturday, March 30. Seward tardily conferred with four or five key senators, including the friendly Californian, Cornelius Cole, who advised him that nothing could be done at so late an hour. Sumner insisted that the treaty be referred to his committee. Since this made instantaneous ratification impossible, President Johnson summoned the Senate in special session for Monday, April 1. The treaty then was read in executive session, reportedly drawing smiles and ridicule from some members, before it went to the Committee on Foreign Relations as Sumner had asked. Sumner informed Seward after the committee met on Monday that the members were strongly adverse, and he forebodingly pressed Stoeckl to withdraw the treaty. The Russian envoy refused this bad advice, while Seward confidently entertained groups of senators, including Sumner, at elegant receptions in his home.[19]

The press, which reported on Seward's "toothsome dinners, meats and drinks" in envious detail, disagreed over the wisdom of purchasing Russian America. Editors floundered at first, their views dimmed by ignorance and twisted by the emotional, partisan politics of Reconstruction. By the end of the Senate debate a majority of editors probably favored the purchase, either for broad expansionist

reasons or because it seemed to be a practical bargain.[20] Finding
information scarce, some even of the newspapers that were opposed
to the purchase published the favorable material that Seward alertly
furnished. These items included laudatory letters to Seward from
naval Commander John Rodgers and Quartermaster General M.C.
Meigs, who had visited Russian America, and a telegram to Secretary of War Edwin Stanton from General Henry W. Halleck. Halleck, commander of the Military Division of the Pacific, called the
cost a "bagatelle" considering the value of the timber and fisheries
and said that westerners would be bitterly disappointed if the treaty
were defeated. Seward also circulated detailed, enthusiastic accounts by Professor Spencer W. Baird of the Smithsonian Institution, which had sent several expeditions to the territory.[21]

Chairman Sumner, the pivotal figure, found it difficult to make
up his mind. He felt aggrieved that Seward had not consulted him
earlier, suspected the secretary of underhanded dealings, and rightly
feared that Seward might rush on to new projects of annexation.
On the other hand, Sumner believed that the United States should
expand northward and thought that the acquisition of Russian
America might advance his dream of obtaining Canada. Several
influential constituents urged him to oppose the treaty, but a larger
number were favorable; so were two scientists whom he respected,
Baird and Harvard Professor Louis Agassiz, who argued that the
small native population meant that there was no problem of annexation without consent. Sumner worried, too, about the reaction of westerners if the treaty were not ratified, and feared that
Russia, considered a longtime friend, would be offended.[22]

Sumner's committee remained divided for several days, except
on criticism of the secretary of state. Two members facetiously
moved to approve the treaty only if Seward were compelled to reside
in Russian America. At this point Sumner grumpily concluded that
the treaty contained slightly more good than ill, and the committee fell in line by a margin of 4 to 2. Five days later, the egotistical
Sumner — warming to the cause and pleased to be acknowledged
the authority on Russian America, which he dubbed "Alaska" from
the Aleut word for the eastern mainland — treated the full Senate
to a speech of almost three hours on the territory's history, resources,
and prospects. (A later published version, filling almost 240 pages
and covering everything from the territory's fossils to its native languages, drew the quip that Sumner had "exhausted the *subject*, as

well as his *readers.*") Snowed under by this verbal blizzard, fellow members paid little apparent heed to Sumner's brief warning that "this treaty must not be a precedent for a system of indiscriminate and costly annexation."[23] Efforts by Senator William Fessenden of Maine to delay a vote failed by 12 to 29, and on April 9 the Senate ratified the Alaska treaty by the deceptively decisive vote of 37 to 2. Stoeckl notified the Department of State on May 15 that his government also had ratified the treaty.

Czar Alexander directed that Stoeckl be thanked and promised him a bonus of 25,000 rubles (worth about $19,000 in gold) with another 5,000 rubles for the secretary of legation, Waldemar Bodisco. Stoeckl considered his reward disappointingly meager, since he had obtained over $2 million more than directed; but he felt relief at the outcome in Washington and wrote exultantly that he planned to bid "an eternal adieu to America the next spring."[24]

Seward at once arranged with his Russian friend for private American ships to sail immediately to Alaskan waters and for Brigadier General L.H. Rousseau to receive the territory. Stoeckl helpfully arranged the necessary directives to Russian authorities in Alaska and even advised American officers on what rations they would need. On October 18, 1867, the Russian flag came down, and an American detachment raised the stars and stripes over the abandoned Russian barracks at Sitka.[25]

By this time the exchange of ratifications of the treaty had taken place. Seward had done everything possible to secure his acquisition, except to obtain the appropriation necessary to pay for the territory. He blithely told Secretary of the Navy Gideon Welles on March 30 that the matter of payment could be dealt with when Congress convened the following winter. Seward received encouragement from prominent Pennsylvania Republican Representative Thaddeus Stevens, who bitterly disliked the President but worked for ratification of the Alaska treaty. "Old Thad" publicly congratulated the secretary of state at the "safe deliverance" following the Senate's action, expressed hope for an easy "afterbirth,"and joined him in assurances to Stoeckl about payment.[26] Such expectations were unwarranted, even in light of what Seward had already accomplished.

Telltale indications of the trouble ahead appeared early. Certain members of the Johnson administration such as Secretary Stanton quietly undercut the purchase as a waste of money, and prominent

newspapers elaborated upon the sketchy reports of senatorial opposition in the secret debates. A few editorial critics were fair-
minded, if occasionally mistaken, and addressed fundamental issues.
One such newspaper was the *New York Sun*, which held that "the
popular American idea about the 'manifest destiny' of this country
contains an element of danger against which we cannot too carefully guard." "Territorial expansion has always been the bane of
nations. . . . Russian America is valueless at best," this paper
reasoned.[27]

Some attacks were politically motivated. Horace Greeley, an un-
remitting enemy of Seward, quickly and with some justification
accused the secretary of seeking to cover up "failures at home." "We
have more territory than we want," Greeley's *New York Tribune*
further complained, and the government will have to borrow money
to purchase this "luxury we are in no condition to afford." The paper
next argued that the price was just the first charge in a continuing
new expense of government. Countering Seward's laudatory publicity, the *Tribune* threw cold water on the secretary's "expensive con-
tinent of ice" and his "rocks and Esquimaux:"

> Mr. Seward's geographical discoveries continue to be telegraphed
> over the country. . . . The climate is delicious, and quite warm in
> Winter; yet the ice fields are inexhaustible, and in the burning heat
> of the Arctic Summer the Esquimaux take refuge in their shade. The
> country is covered with pine forests, and vegetable gardens flourish
> along the coast, whereon the walrus are also found in vast multitudes.
> Wheat, Seals, Barley, White Bears, Turnips, Icebergs, Whales, and
> Gold Mines, are found as far north as the sixtieth degree. . . . All
> tastes are gratified in Mr. Seward's land, which is not Russian Amer-
> ica, but Utopia. On paper it is a wonderful country; on ice it is what
> is generally called a big thing.[28]

Other newspapers, including several that favored the acquisition,
fired similar scornful barrages. "There are Senators, as it appears,"
the *New York Herald* claimed, "who are not willing to pay seven
millions of dollars for an ice house, a worthless desert with which
to enable the Secretary of State to cover up the thousand mortifica-
tions and defeats he has suffered with the shipwrecked Southern
policy of Andrew Johnson." Even the annexationist *New York World*
ridiculed the farfetched claims of the territory's advocates in a series
of humorous headlines:

Tropical Disadvantages Set Off
by the Value of the Ice Trade

Secretary Seward's New Ice-other-mal Line

A Great Opening for Soda-Water Fountains
and Skating Ponds

Ice-Cream — Ice Bergs

Seward's newspaper supporters responded to these jokes with barely suppressed laughter and solemn rebuttal.[29]

Historians have quoted fondly the amusing editorial jibes at "Walrussia," but they have ignored the concurrent journalistic hints of corrupt activities. The suspicion of corruption echoed the persistent rhetoric and revealed a basic theme of American politics, as well as the momentary opportunism of the press; and it had great significance during the prolonged controversy after 1867 over the Alaska issue. One of the first suggestions of scandal appeared on April 1 in Washington and Chicago dispatches, published also in Philadelphia and San Francisco, that there would be a congressional investigation "to ascertain the origin of the scheme and what is behind it. Nobody believes that the whole $7,000,000 will go into Russian coffers." A day later the *New York World* probed another crevasse by asserting that the cession was "one of the very neatest operations of Russian diplomacy."[30]

Greeley's *Tribune*, the purchase's most severe opponent, picked up these lines of argument within a week. It first mocked Seward's "Russian treaty dinner parties" and accused him of "employing the machinery of the Associated Press" and of sending a thousand-word telegram, costing the government 75 cents a word, "to persons in California and other states" where sentiment favored the treaty. The paper further charged that Seward had been aided by "the regular Washington Lobby, reenforced by some of the most skillful graduates of Fagin's [Thurlow Weed's] Albany Institute," who are interested only in money. On April 9 the *Tribune* reported on "another dinner party for Esquimaux Senators" and referred to "the 'Esquimaux ring.'"[31] Similar references to Seward's "Esquimaux stews and ices, his California wines and Kentucky Bourbon, his seven millions and the lobby" appeared in the *New York Herald* on the same day. Neither Seward nor his allies bothered to respond to any of these vague charges of corruption. On April 10 the *Trib-*

une unhappily conceded ratification of "the little job." Critical editorial opinion then largely ceased. The journalistic basis, however, had been established for the major scandal that eventually erupted.[32]

Neither the House nor the Senate pursued the newspaper suggestions of wrongdoing over Alaska in the spring of 1867, but Congress's antagonism toward the Johnson administration was ripening rapidly. At the very moment that the Senate debated the Alaska treaty, the House Judiciary Committee combed reports and rumors about Johnson and even reviewed his private bank accounts to find grounds for a charge of "high crimes and misdemeanors." There were aspersions of adultery, while Representative Ben Butler of Massachusetts publicly insinuated Johnson's complicity with John Wilkes Booth in Lincoln's assassination. On June 1, 1867, the committee voted 5 to 4 that there was no basis for impeachment, but it continued to take testimony. Bitter controversy over the appointment of military governors in the Southern states ensued during the summer of 1867.

Blissfully ignoring these harsh realities, the ebullient Seward agreed in July 1867 to purchase Denmark's Caribbean islands of St. Thomas and St. John, over which he had been dallying with the Danish minister since 1865.[33] Simultaneously he responded to Robert J. Walker's suggestion that the United States also purchase Greenland and Iceland from the Danes by asking that practiced pamphleteer to compile "facts on the subject, that they might be on the files of the department and ready for use whenever the question might be considered hereafter by the government." Several months later, Walker submitted his report, based on a study by the United States Coast Survey; and Seward ordered that it be printed with an introduction by Walker.[34] Fortunately for this insatiable duo, and for the Alaska treaty, the report on Greenland and Iceland did not become known for almost a year. Meanwhile, on October 24, 1867, the treaty to purchase St. Thomas and St. John for $7.5 million was concluded in Copenhagen. Soon thereafter a hurricane swept St. Thomas, followed by a tidal wave that washed the *U.S.S. Monongahela* high onto the island, and reports came in of an earthquake on nearby St. Croix, another Danish island.

Seward and Walker continued to pursue their latest pipedreams, barely flinching before the blows of nature and the ridicule of cynical journalists such as Bret Harte and Mark Twain. An equally undaunted President Johnson transmitted a copy of the Alaska treaty to Congress on July 6, 1867. He invited attention "to the subject of an appropriation for this payment" and to the need for an occupation and territorial government.[35] The message was not even read in the Senate until July 16, when it was referred to the Appropriations Committee, and in the House until July 19, when it was referred to the Committee on Foreign Affairs. The following day, Congress adjourned until November 21, 1867.

Before the recess occurred, Representative Nathaniel Banks of Massachusetts, the chairman of the Foreign Affairs Committee, and Senator Henry Wilson, also of Massachusetts, presented a petition from the widow Anna B. Perkins, "Praying that out of the sums of money to be paid to the Imperial Government of Russia, under the terms of the recent treaty between that Government and the United States, there shall be suspended or withheld a sum sufficient to pay the claim of the late B.W. Perkins."[36] The Perkins claim had been an irritant in Russian-American relations since 1855 — and it remained so until the Senate finally interred it in 1886. From the beginning Stoeckl's personal integrity was at issue. The claim had no inherent connection with the acquisition of Alaska, but it helped to delay passage of the appropriation for a full year after July 1867. The Perkins affair was the work of more than a half-dozen opportunistic lawyers, lobbyists, journalists, and congressmen who shrewdly entangled the claim with the treaty. The consequences were nearly to jeopardize the purchase and to fatten the issue of corruption involving Alaska.

The claim dated back to the Crimean War, when the Russian government looked abroad for war supplies. Captain Benjamin W. Perkins, a resident of Worcester, Massachusetts, claimed that he had made an oral agreement and a provisional written contract with Stoeckl and with various Russian agents whom the minister had referred to him for 154 tons of powder and from 30,000 to 35,000 rifles. Perkins was to purchase and ship the materiel, assuming all risks of seizure by England as contraband, with 100 percent profit promised. He stated that he had made the powder ready and obtained the rifles from a vendor but had shipped none of the munitions when the war ended and the Russian agents forgot their commitments. Perkins asserted that he had suffered a loss of $370,000, plus interest. A New York court dismissed the first of the claims, awarding Perkins $200; but he pressed the matter in Congress and with the Department of State. Secretary Cass submitted the claim in 1860 to the Russian government, which refused flatly to consider it. Stoeckl disowned one of the agents and denied vehemently that he had ever made any agreement with Perkins. Secretary Seward took the view that oral agreements were valid in the United States and pursued the case intermittently until 1867 through the United States minister in Russia. Minister Clay, who considered the claim unjustified, sought a settlement for $130,000 in 1863; but the claimants' lawyer, Joseph B. Stewart, refused the offer. Following Perkins's death, his widow pressed the claim with the support of such influential congressmen as Banks, Wilson, Butler, and Stevens and the formidable lawyer-lobbyists Joseph Stewart and Simon Stevens — a protege but not a relative of Representative Thaddeus Stevens.[37]

Stoeckl, sensing danger to his Alaska project and prospects for personal rewards, warned Seward early in September that the Perkins claim would be revived after Congress reconvened on November 21:

> I do not know, my dear Sir, whether you are aware that some persons in this country, who are interested in a pretended and stale claim against the Russian government, called the 'Perkins claim,' are proposing to ask Congress to withhold a portion of the consideration money of the Russian treaty, for the purpose of gratifying that claim. Rumors of this design may perhaps reach St. Petersburg and cause some uneasiness there. I hope you will not think me wrong in alluding to this matter.

The secretary replied calmly on September 11: "I do not think that in any case the Government of the United States will fail to fulfil the stipulations contained in the Russian American treaty to the letter as well as in spirit, and I think that you may, without hesitation, so assure the Cabinet at St. Petersburg."[38]

Seward's policies received two new blows in Congress, however, even before the spectre of the Perkins claim reappeared. On November 25, the House of Representatives approved by a vote of 93 to 43 a resolution by Cadwallader C. Washburn of Wisconsin against "further purchases of territory." This measure was aimed at the recent treaty to acquire the Danish "earthquake islands" of St. Thomas and St. John, which aroused little enthusiasm either in Congress or the press. But Washburn hinted that he would oppose "Walrussia" as well.[39] Five days later, Alaska again came into question when the House adopted unanimously a motion by Halbert E. Paine, also from Wisconsin, requesting that the Judiciary Committee report whether "Congress has the right to grant or refuse, at its discretion, an appropriation for the payment stipulated" in the treaty with Russia.[40]

President Johnson countered these congressional opponents by announcing in his annual message on December 3 that the Senate soon would receive the treaty with Denmark for St. Thomas and St. John. He also reminded the members that there was unfinished business involving Russia, observing coolly: "It will hardly be necessary to call the attention of Congress to the subject of providing for the payment to Russia of the sum stipulated." He recalled further that the United States had taken formal possession of Alaska, which would remain under military occupation until Congress provided a civil government.[41]

Adding to the administration's troubles, there were reports that an attempt would be made in Congress to resurrect the Perkins claim and to charge it against the Alaska payment. Stoeckl angrily portrayed this idea as a fraud and a conspiracy, informing his government that the lawyers and congressmen advocating the claim had made an agreement for a total of $800,000, from which they would obtain three-fourths and Mrs. Perkins the remainder. Ben Butler, he maintained, is "interested for $30,000 in the Perkins swindle."[42] Stoeckl also reported, however, that he had gained a convert. Seward persuaded Chairman Thaddeus Stevens of the Appropriations Committee, champion both of Alaska and the Perkins claim, to oppose Butler's obstructive amendments. During floor debate on December 9, Butler, who was apparently unaware of Stevens's shift, moved to refer the bill to the Appropriations Committee rather than to Foreign Affairs under Chairman Banks, who strongly favored the Alaska appropriation and had altered tactics on the claim. Butler did enjoy the support of prestigious Illinois Representative Elihu B. Washburne—hometown friend of General Ulysses S. Grant, the leading presidential prospect, and brother of Wisconsin Representative Cadwallader Washburn—who scorned the purchase of this "worthless territory." (The brothers spelled their surname differently.) But Banks throttled Butler's maneuvers, and Stevens replied firmly: "When the Constitution, which is the paramount law of the land, declares that we owe a debt, I should be ashamed to refuse to pay it." The House narrowly rejected Butler's amendment, by a vote of 73 to 82, and voted almost concurrently against a resolution to impeach the President.[43]

The appropriation for Alaska faced continued opposition in Congress, however, including increased impetus for impeachment. On December 19, the House sought to stall on Alaska by asking Johnson for all the papers of the negotiation. The President transmitted Seward's highly selective compilation on February 17, just a week before Congress voted decisively to proceed with impeachment. The secretary of state claimed that the Alaska treaty probably stood alone in the annals of diplomacy for being concluded without "protocols or despatches." He included Sumner's massive "speech" and other paeans of praise in his report but ingenuously omitted all explicit references to the Perkins claim.[44]

Early in 1868, Representative Halbert E. Paine of Wisconsin called for the papers on the Perkins claim.[45] William Kelley of Pennsylvania introduced still another resolution about the Perkins claim in February. Kelley, moreover, acted on behalf of Thad Stevens, who was busy with Butler and others readying the case of the House of Representatives for prosecution on the impeachment charges against President Johnson.[46] After the President submitted the bulky documents on the Perkins claim, there was a sharp argument in the House over whether to print them. The papers were sent to the Committee on Foreign Affairs but not printed, after Godlove Orth of Indiana argued persuasively that the claim had nothing to do with the purchase of Alaska.[47]

The news from the territory, meanwhile, was no help to Alaska's advocates. Washington newspapers reported that the Americans at Sitka, experiencing their first northern winter, suffered threats from Indians whose liquor the army had confiscated, burglaries, brutal fights, and temperatures "110° below the freezing point." To offset all the objections, the administration lobbied intensively, further establishing the basis for later charges of wrongdoing. Seward, who was still confident about the chances for Alaska though not for the Danish islands, conferred frequently with Robert J. Walker after Congress reconvened and urged his Democratic friend to prepare another expansionist argument. Walker responded with three lengthy articles, jointly entitled the "Letter of Hon. R.J. Walker on the Annexation of Alaska and St. Thomas." The pieces appeared on January 28, 29, and 30, 1868, in Washington's most prominent Republican paper, the *Daily Morning Chronicle*, whose proprietor and editor was Walker's close friend, Colonel John W. Forney. The *Chronicle* briefly had questioned the Russian treaty but shifted ground by April 9, 1867, upon Senate ratification. Forney, who simultaneously published the *Philadelphia Press*, bitterly opposed the Johnson administration's southern policies. His papers relentlessly advocated the conviction of President Johnson during the trial that began in the Senate in March 1868. Forney also had served since July 1861 as secretary of the Senate, a position that he held until June 4, 1868, shortly after the impeachment trial ended.[48] His intimacy with such leading radical Republicans as Stevens and Sumner magnified the importance of his publication of Walker's articles. Portions of the letters also appeared in other influential papers, and Walker — as was his custom — had them printed as a pamphlet. He gave Seward 1,000 free copies and took 9,000 copies himself.[49]

Several scholars have asserted that Walker was in financial distress and in danger of losing his home under a legal judgment, and that he wrote these articles in the employ of the Danish and Russian ministers. The established facts are that wealthy retired Washington banker W.W. Corcoran had saved his old friend Walker's home a year earlier but that Walker remained in debt to him.[50] It is possible that Walker received a retainer or reward from Denmark. The Danish minister — describing Walker as a man without office but not insignificant politically — delightedly sent copies of the letters to his foreign office. This was the extent of Walker's advocacy of the Danish islands. Walker told Seward at the time, moreover, that he was having copies of the articles printed at his "own expense," and he denied subsequently to a congressional committee that he had previously been a counsel for either Denmark or Russia.[51]

As for Russian influence, the contents of the articles belie a subsidy from Stoeckl at this stage of affairs and suggest another explanation for their authorship. Walker devoted only one paragraph of the first letter to praise of Alaska's climate, harbors, and timber. He maintained in a second paragraph that the territory was chiefly significant for supremacy of the Pacific and as a step toward the acquisition of British Columbia. Most of the first letter consisted of an historical argument that the safety of the Republic against England and other dangers of "disintegration, secession, and disunion" lay in "the maintenance, perpetuation, and extension of the Union." The other two long letters used similar arguments on behalf of acquiring St. Thomas and St. John islands. In all likelihood, these extraordinary documents represented Walker's genuine enthusiasm for "annexation in every quarter, north, south, east, and west."[52] At the same time, the letters identified Walker to the press, politicians, and the public as the leading advocate of Seward's policy of expansion and described one of the planks he favored for the Democrats in the approaching election of 1868.

Stoeckl sensed that the enthusiastic Walker might be useful in winning support in Congress for the Alaska appropriation, which was due Russia on April 20, 1868. He needed help, especially because of the growing impeachment sentiment and the tactics of the Perkins claimants. Stoeckl took pride in knowing how to deal with influential congressmen, however, and for the moment he worked through Chairman Banks by means of correspondence and meetings in New York City and Washington.[53]

The Perkins lobbyists also approached Banks.[54] In addition, the byzantine-minded Secretary Seward sent Simon Stevens, the Perkins attorney, to see Banks on behalf of *Alaska!*[55] Banks already shared Seward's enthusiasm for expansion, and he busily gathered information to be used in the approaching debate. Before he was ready to act, the issue erupted briefly on the floor of the House of Representatives. On March 14, William Higby, a new member from California, pleaded that Alaska's prospects were impressive and that the House must consider Russian views as well as its own sentiment. Cadwallader Washburn interrupted him with his familiar charge that the area was valueless.[56] Four days later, Banks tested sentiment in the smaller crucible of his own committee, arguing that it was "the duty of Congress" to pass the appropriation. After General Elihu Washburne responded that the bill should not be enacted because of the government's depleted finances and Alaska's worthlessness, the committee put off further discussion until May. The *New York Tribune* reported that the committee was evenly divided but concluded hopefully that the opponents might yet defeat it.[57] Banks at once notified Seward that the members had informally agreed to wait until the impeachment trial in the Senate was at an end and that the delay was not the result of opposition to the bill. "My opinion," he declared, "is that the Committee will report in favor of the payment" and that it would receive House approval.[58]

President Johnson, who was distracted and intensely worried over the Senate impeachment proceedings, viewed Alaska's prospects pessimistically. Seward, in contrast, informed Stoeckl of the situation in Banks's committee and confidently described the judgment of its chairman as "altogether reliable."[59] Stoeckl became depressed despite Seward's assurances, and, as days passed without congressional action, he suggested cynically to St. Petersburg that it shame the United States by offering the territory for nothing. Gorchakov replied that this might tempt "American cupidity" and recommended instead a diplomatic note. He also agreed that the United States might delay in making payment.[60]

General Banks did even better than he had predicted. His committee reported favorably on the appropriation bill for Alaska on May 18, just a few days before the impeachment trial ended in the Senate. Floor debate on the Alaska measure would begin at the end of June, between the Republican and Democratic conventions. It is important to keep in mind that congressional action on the appropriation for Alaska not only converged with the controversy over impeachment, as historians have often noted, but also with the intense campaign for the Democratic presidential nomination and with the election of 1868.

While the appropriation bill was still in Banks's committee, Stoeckl quietly employed several agents to advance the measure in Congress. He cautioned the secretary of state, and President Johnson through Seward, to remain discreetly in the background. (Johnson had been considering a special message.) Stoeckl explained to Gorchakov that he and Seward were acting "together" upon members of Congress through the "intervention" of "lawyers" and "influential men," such as Robert J. Walker, in whom he expressed full confidence.[61]

Walker was an old acquaintance of the Russian envoy, who approached him in May upon Seward's advice. Stoeckl flattered the Democratic elder statesman by praising his January pamphlet and engaged him as counsel with a promised retainer of $20,000 gold. Walker took as his associate counsel Frederick P. Stanton, a former congressman and familiar Washington political figure. The relationship between Walker and Stanton was a long-standing one, and it had been cemented by intense political experiences. Walker and Stanton had been cronies since the administration of Polk, when Stanton served the first of his five terms as an expansionist Democratic representative from Tennessee. In 1857 President Buchanan and Walker, the newly appointed governor of Kansas Territory, persuaded Stanton to give up his law practice in Washington and become territorial secretary. By an understanding with the President, Stanton often served as acting governor in place of Walker, who absented himself frequently on political and business errands. The duo soon drew the fire of Southerners for exposing the election frauds of pro-slavery elements in Kansas. In December 1857 Buchanan had removed Stanton as acting governor after he convened the free-soil territorial legislature. Governor Walker, then in Washington, re-signed in protest a few days later, and both men moved into the political camp of Senator Stephen A. Douglas, where they remained until the inauguration of Abraham Lincoln.[62]

When Stoeckl hired the services of Walker and Stanton, he also obtained the latter's coadjutor, Robert W. Latham. Latham earlier had come to public attention during the Buchanan administration. He then occupied the position of business manager for Secretary of War John B. Floyd, whose service ended in scandal and abrupt resignation. Latham was talked of at the time as a man with con-nections to New York speculators and contractors, and as a lobbyist who bought votes. Ten years later, in Alaska days, the shadowy Latham described himself as a New Jersey railroad man and pos-sessed a reputation in Washington as a specialist in pressing claims.

Latham also was known on Capitol Hill as a friend of Andrew Johnson. During the impeachment trial he served as an emissary to Johnson for two Republican senators, Samuel Pomeroy of Kan-sas and William Stewart of Nevada. Pomeroy, who viewed im-peachment as a political question, asked Latham on March 15, 1868, to tell the President that he could only avoid conviction by dismiss-ing the entire cabinet and installing Nathaniel Banks as secretary of state, Robert J. Walker as secretary of the treasury, and Freder-ick P. Stanton as secretary of the navy. Latham, who probably helped to invent the scheme, left the plan at the Executive Man-sion the next day. Johnson rejected the idea, but he continued to use Latham as one of his agents. In July 1868 Latham attended the Democratic national convention with a small party of Johnson's in-timates to work for the President's candidacy. From New York City he urged Johnson to remove Secretary of the Treasury Hugh Mc-Culloch, whom he saw as a barrier to nomination. After the con-vention, Latham proposed to New York State Democratic chair-man Samuel Tilden that he bribe Washington reporters to support the Democratic nominees, Horatio Seymour and Frank P. Blair, Jr.[63] Latham's claim that he could purchase the services of the Washington press corps during the election of 1868, if Tilden furnished enough money, must be kept in mind as the story of the Alaska scandal unfolds. Latham's connections with politicians and correspondents in Washington lay behind the controversy that aroused Congress to investigate the affair in late 1868.

A few words more are necessary in order to understand the full scope of the political machinations of Walker, Stanton, and Latham in mid-1868. These indefatigable operators explored every opportunity. Before the Democratic convention, Walker, as will be seen, initially favored General Winfield S. Hancock, but he shifted to Chief Justice Salmon P. Chase. Stanton chaired Chase's Committee of One Hundred and served as his campaign treasurer. Latham, as noted above, was one of President Johnson's agents. Subsequently, Walker and Latham were in contact with Tilden, who was Seymour's friend and campaign manager, and with other intimates of the Democratic nominee.

Tilden had called on Walker shortly before the Democratic convention. On a visit to Washington in May the wealthy New York Democrat consulted Governor Walker about "who ought to be nominated by the Democratic convention for the Presidency." Walker pondered the problem created by the Republican candidacy of General Ulysses S. Grant and on May 30 wrote Tilden at length on behalf of General Hancock. He reminded Tilden as well of the need for "a curb upon the frenzy of the House," where the recent failure of impeachment sparked a furor. (The Alaska appropriation bill awaited action in this chamber.) A Republican congressional victory, with the "addition of 20 members from the Negro-ized South," would create more trouble, Walker advised Tilden. His racist comment typified the thinking of leading Democrats during the campaign of 1868.[64]

In the battle for Alaska, which continued simultaneously, Walker prepared further materials for the press. He enjoyed this activity, for it was his pastime to glean information from encyclopedias and to use what he found for political purposes. He composed a pamphlet, which was printed by the *Washington Daily National Intelligencer*, and seven long articles, which appeared with minor alterations as editorials in the Democratic *Intelligencer* and in the Republican *Daily Morning Chronicle*. The articles were unsigned but bore Walker's unmistakable imprint.[65]

The first piece, a detailed account of Alaska's fisheries, appeared in the *Chronicle* on June 24. Two more editorials followed on June 27, the day that Banks opened debate on the floor of the House. One was a characteristically sweeping manifesto on the value of Polk's territorial acquisitions and the prospects for extending "the progressive spirit of the age" to a China and Japan that were opening their doors to the world. The second editorial spoke of obligations to Russia, China's employment of the popular Republican Anson Burlingame as a diplomat, and the certain doom of any party that opposed extension of the Union.[66] Other articles followed at appropriate moments, circumnavigating Alaskan topics from Vitus Behring's discoveries and the possible Asian extension of Christianity to the importance of the Pacific-coast vote for the Republican party. A humorous editorial, teasing New England's "codfish aristocracy" and advising prairie members that there was "nothing better than salmon and cod to recuperate brain waste," shrewdly provided diversion from the serious arguments.[67] Seward's hand appeared, too, in a San Francisco letter that was published in several papers during the debate, reporting that gold had been found in Alaska. This is "a very important letter," Colonel Forney editorialized.[68]

Secretary Seward counted eighty sure votes as the showdown on the Alaska bill approached. "All the Democrats are counted for voting the money," reported the *New York Sun*'s correspondent Uriah Painter, who believed that the addition of a minority of Republicans might be enough to pass the appropriation.[69] Painter himself was to emerge later as a central figure in the congressional investigation of the events he now described. Banks exuded more confidence than did even the secretary of state, writing Seward on June 27 that he counted 117 votes for the bill. Conceding "many others" doubtful, Banks moved ahead circumspectly.[70] At the outset of debate he informed the House that his committee would not approve withholding the Perkins claim against the appropriation but that it favored a resolution prepared by the claimants; he would recommend it for passage as a separate issue. He also agreed to delay opening discussion of the appropriation until C.C. Washburn could be present.[71]

Banks's speech opening the debate was able, though his remarks were familiar. He stressed Russia's friendly acts, Alaska's importance as "the key" to control of the Pacific, and the value of the timber, fisheries, and other resources, which he prophesied perspicaciously would provide, when "fully developed, employment for two hundred and fifty thousand persons." He offered one new enticement—anticipating the stories planted in the press—a report that gold had been found "at Cook's inlet, on the Stikine river."[72]

C.C. Washburn, who skeptically interrupted Banks to question his claim of gold, led the rebuttal. His first contentions likewise echoed previous debates: the territory had no value; there would be endless expense in governing the natives; and the American people had not asked for the treaty, which was "secretly negotiated." Then he opened a new salient. As *New York Sun* reporter Uriah Painter had predicted a day before, on June 29, Washburn adopted the argument "that the House has the right to refuse the appropriation." Raising this constitutional issue allowed him to attract members who favored a greater role for the House in foreign affairs as well as to exploit the widespread distrust of Seward. "Pass this appropriation," Washburn warned, and "it will be but a few days before you will hear of the ratification by the Senate of the treaty for the purchase of St. Thomas." Nor did Seward's designs stop there. "No sir. I believe a treaty is now being negotiated with Denmark for the purchase of Greenland and Iceland."

Skeptical laughter rippled through the chamber. "Well, gentlemen, laugh at it," Washburn responded. "I tell gentlemen who go for Alaska that Greenland to-day is a better purchase." Excited and somewhat confused, Washburn said again that he expected further expansionist schemes. Then he blurted out that Robert J. Walker was involved:

> I have had placed upon my table since I began to speak to-day some pages of a document now printing at the Government Printing Office for the State Department, which shows that the purchase of Greenland is in contemplation. . . . I have but a few leaves of the document, and have not had time to look even at them. But upon glancing over them at this moment I observe a letter from Robert J. Walker, who figures wherever there is any territory to be bought, or any money to be appropriated to pay for it.[73]

One historian of the Alaska affair has labelled Washburn's references to Greenland and Iceland a "fictitious story" supplied by correspondent Painter in an attempt to defeat the appropriation.[74] In fact, Washburn's disclosure about Seward's plans was entirely correct. As for Painter, he did help to reveal Seward's scheme, but not for the reason that Walker and his cronies very shortly suggested—

that the correspondent had unsuccessfully sought a share of the payment to Russia. Nor is it true that Painter was simply a disinterested investigative reporter intent on exposing wrongdoing, as he claimed.[75]

Another detour is necessary at this point, so that Uriah Painter's part in the plot is fully known. The reporter's original role actually was very modest, but it led to other inquiries and to the first revelations of the Alaska scandal, which eventually ensnared him in turn. Painter was no innocent in the polished marble corridors of Capitol Hill, but a man of more moment than many contemporaries realized or than any historian has yet recorded. A Washington reporter since 1860 for the *Philadelphia Inquirer* as well as the *New York Sun*, he was a lobbyist simultaneously.[76] The fact that Painter and other Washington correspondents practiced a second profession was little known at the time and remains so, in part because both editors and politicians covered up their activities.

In 1868 Painter was Washington representative for a number of the nation's most prominent financiers and businessmen, among them Jay Cooke & Company; Thomas A. Scott, vice-president of the Pennsylvania Railroad, who was soon to take over the Union Pacific, the Texas and Pacific, and other railroads; W.W. Harding, publisher of the *Philadelphia Inquirer*, and I.W. England, publisher of the *New York Sun*. (Painter himself was systematically acquiring stock in the *Sun*.) By 1871, perhaps some months earlier, Painter enjoyed a close relationship with Oakes Ames of Credit Mobilier, the construction company for the Union Pacific Railroad, whose profits were then enormous and whose reputation still was unscathed. All the while, Painter bought and sold stocks mostly of the Western Union Company, and his personal financial records showed healthy if modest balances. Within a few years, Painter was in a position to build railroads on Maryland's eastern shore, acquire theaters, develop some of the nation's first telephone companies, and finance the early enterprises of Thomas Alva Edison.[77]

In 1868, Painter's political intimates, mostly anti-Johnson Republicans, were equally impressive: Senator Roscoe Conkling of New York; Senator Ben Wade of Ohio, the president pro tem of the Senate until March 1869 and the man who would have become President of the United States had Johnson been convicted; Representative John Covode of Pennsylvania, who also published the *Congressional*

Globe; William E. Chandler of New Hampshire, secretary of the Republican National Committee and leading organizer of Grant's campaigns in 1868 and 1872; and Galusha Grow, wartime speaker of the House, veteran congressman, and chairman of the Pennsylvania Union Republican State Central Committee. Painter worked closely with Grow for Grant's election in 1868 and later spoke freely for Grow in dealings with Chandler over patronage in the Philadelphia navy yard. To complete his spiderweb of Washington ventures, Painter also held the position of clerk of the House Committee on Post Offices and Post Roads, where many favors were dispensed.[78]

Sun editor Charles A. Dana attempted to keep his influential reporter on a regular tether. He constantly urged Painter to wire his reports earlier, shorten his stories, pursue the topics that interested Dana, and focus on "giving the news . . . Ours is *not* a partisan paper, & I don't wish to have a partisan view taken of any subject." Dana, however, cautioned Painter not to write stories critical of William Evarts, one of Johnson's counsels during the trial and soon to become attorney general, because Evarts was a stockholder of the *Sun*.[79] After the nomination of Governor Seymour, moreover, the *Sun* supported his candidacy and described itself as "the leading Democratic paper of the United States," only to concede by September that Grant would win and that Seymour should withdraw.[80] Painter worked closely with Dana and publisher England, who paid him extra for special reports and frequently called on him to guard the newspaper's legislative interests.[81]

Where did Painter stand on Alaska? In 1867, when Seward first revealed his treaty, Painter favored acquiring this "vast territory" for "a merely nominal sum." He later claimed that he had opposed the treaty from the outset, telling the House investigating committee that he took this position because he had heard Senator Sumner ridicule it.[82] The supple correspondent more likely changed from support initially to opposition later, doing so because the *Sun* opposed the purchase and the ideas of Manifest Destiny.[83] The *Sun* did not belabor Seward's purchase, however, and Dana accepted the fact as 1868 wore on that Congress must appropriate the money for Alaska. When debate on the appropriations bill began on June 30, 1868, the *Sun* repeated Painter's prediction that the measure would pass and conceded that the United States should pay for the territory it occupied. Dana insisted, though, that "limits" be established on the power of the Executive and the Senate to acquire "some similar purchase in the future."[84]

Now we resume the narrative of events. In late June 1868, just prior to the opening of debate in the House, Painter learned from Washburn that he, Butler, Shelby Cullom of Illinois, and other opponents of the treaty would raise the issue of limits on executive power. In return for this advance information about the opponents' stand, Painter told Washburn that Seward was planning to acquire Greenland and Iceland. Washburn at first was incredulous. Painter knew of the pamphlet by Walker being published in the Government Printing Office, however, and he persuaded Washburn to send for proof sheets, which arrived in the middle of his speech.[85] Simultaneously Painter sent the *Sun* a dispatch, which was published on July 1, that Seward had "nearly completed negotiations for the purchase of Greenland and Iceland." The secretary had obtained promises of "sufficient support in the Senate," Painter asserted, and was having a special report on these territories published at the Government Printing Office.[86]

Robert Walker, unfazed by Washburn's criticisms and the *Sun's* alarms, left Washington on July 2 for the Democratic convention in New York City. Before he departed, he wrote Seward that he had done all he could in Washington. Predicting that even the *New York Tribune* would support the appropriation, he expressed hope that the Democratic party would put Alaska on its banner. (His prediction about the *Tribune* was safe enough, since Greeley had editorialized three days earlier, on June 30, that it was "rather late now to reject the bargain" even though Seward's action was regrettable.) Walker urged the secretary and the President to insure the votes of every Democratic congressman because Alaska, even more than the President's "immortal" vetoes, was "the great act of his administration" and will insure "ultimately, the political and commercial control of the world."[87] In New York, Walker appeared prominently on the stage at the Democratic presidential nominating convention in newly erected Tammany Hall and urged upon his party a platform of peaceful expansion. The Democratic party, he proclaimed, deserved the entire credit for extension of the Union.[88]

Chairman Banks repeatedly delayed final action on the Alaska appropriation during the Democrats' prolonged convention. He did not wish to risk acting without them and used the time to obtain opinions on the opposition's arguments against the exclusive treaty-making power of the President and Senate. There was an unquestioned obligation to appropriate money for a treaty, one authority wrote him.[89] Banks prepared to accept a verbal compromise. He received encouragement on the measure's general prospects from the Boston Customs House, one of his patronage strongholds, where a political lieutenant expressed confidence that Banks would carry the appropriation bill and become "MINISTER TO RUSSIA." The possibility of this appointment, a topic of speculation in political circles during early July, whetted Banks's interest.[90]

During the Democrats' absence, on July 7, General Butler again assailed the appropriation. Himself an expansionist, Butler hypocritically decried the "spread-eagleism, the filibusteringism, and the manifest destinyism." Still resentful of the fact that Seward had ordered him relieved from duty in New Orleans during the Civil War, he spoke insultingly of the secretary of state. Only Seward, he said, was "insane enough to buy the earthquakes in St. Thomas and ice-fields in Greenland" as well as Alaska. The United States might have had that "land, or rather the ice," for the asking and would do well to return it to the Czar if Russia's friendship were at stake. At last he reached his point: $500,000 should be withheld for the Perkins "widow and orphans." Banks at once declared his friend's amendment out of order, and the Chair concurred. Butler vainly appealed the ruling but lost for lack of quorum.[91]

Full debate resumed on Monday, July 13, as the weary Democrats drifted back to Washington after requiring twenty-two ballots to nominate Governor Seymour. One speech on the Alaska measure followed another, with little new said. Anti-Johnson radicals again were prominent in the opposition. Banks decisively beat back a further effort by Butler on July 14 to set aside $500,000 for the Perkins claim. The presiding officer once more ruled the amendment not germane, and the House sustained him by 93 to 27.[92]

While Washington steamed in temperatures well above 100°, Robert J. Walker, Russian Secretary Bodisco, and their associates spent Tuesday afternoon on the floor of the House reminding members of the advantages of polar ices and other Alaskan assets. "If only for cooling the imagination" quipped the still hostile *New York Tribune*, "it must have seemed dog cheap." The press also reported the conspicuous presence of Walker and his allies and their ecstatic pleasure over the bill's approval by a wide margin. The final tally, which fell just four votes shy of Banks's original count of 117, was 113 to 43. The opponents included C.C. Washburn, Butler, and thirty-nine others who had voted earlier for Johnson's impeachment. Forty-four members did not vote.[93]

On the eve of this satisfying victory, Walker's assistant, Robert Latham, recognized an opportunity to capitalize upon the developing shape of affairs at the Capitol. Latham wrote confidently to Samuel Tilden, who had already taken charge of the Seymour presidential campaign, about what the Democrats might accomplish with the Washington press corps. This revealing letter, which was only mentioned earlier, now must be quoted in its entirety:

> I tried to see you before leaving New York last week, but failed to do so.
>
> It is vastly important for you to have the Reporters of the press in this City, who make the views, and give the tone to every important Newspaper in the Country. They are now in an organized State, and if *done at once* can be controled for Seymour & Blair.
>
> The Grant men have declined to pay them any money but offer *largely in case of Success*! This don't Suit.
>
> It will take about 3,000 to 3,500$ per month until the Campaign is over to Secure these men about 30 in number, and they are worth more than all the Stump orators in the field and if I had the Control would pay them *if necessary* 10,000$ p month or So much as would Secure them.
>
> There are no Such men in this Country, as the Reporters stationed here for energy, and Smartness.
>
> If you can get Gov. F.P. Stanton *upon whose letter head* I write, to take charge of the money, and disburse it, you must succeed. Gov Stanton is Treasury of the Chase Committee here. He is brother-inlaw of Mr. Perrin who was Secretary of your convention.
>
> Cant you come or Send Some reliable man here at once, to attend to this mater.
>
> Let them call on Stanton who is posted.
>
>   Your friend
>   R.W. Latham[94]

A few historians have mentioned this letter in connection with the election of 1868. No one has linked it with lobbying for the appropriation to purchase Alaska, and its importance has not been recognized. The frank document provides evidence that Latham and Stanton were buying, or claiming to buy, the services of Washington reporters, and the Alaska appropriation was the only concurrent major public issue. They were unquestionably seeking to participate in and profit from the Seymour political campaign. The passing reference to a "Mr. Perrin" is a revealing detail, for it lays open more of the Walker-Stanton political organization. Edwin O. Perrin, then of Brooklyn but formerly a Tennessean like his brother-in-law Stanton, was a well-known orator who had been part of the carefully selected entourage of Walker and Stanton in Kansas Territory in 1857.[95] As for Walker himself, he recently had been in touch with Tilden about Democratic prospects and in all likelihood knew of his close associates' expanded activities. It would have been virtually impossible for him not to do so because of what followed from Latham's letter.

Samuel Tilden certainly knew of the ties between Walker and Stanton. In the course of following Tilden's response to Stanton and Latham, we shall meet the Wood brothers of New York for the first time. Democratic Representative Fernando Wood was the corrupt former mayor of New York City; his equally unprincipled brother Benjamin was publisher and editor of the Democratic *New York Daily News*, a former congressman, currently a New York state senator, and, with Tilden, one of the organizers of the Seymour draft. After Tilden received one or more letters from Latham, he sent to Washington his friend and associate Colonel John Dash Van Buren, who was also a trusted friend of both Horatio Seymour and Salmon P. Chase. Van Buren was to consult with the representatives of the defeated Democratic presidential hopefuls, including President Johnson and the supporters of Hancock and Chase. Van Buren visited Latham, who conversed with him and introduced him to the proprietors of the *Washington Daily National Intelligencer*, which Tilden had subsidized. Latham informed one of the Woods on July 20 that Van Buren had "made a most unfavorable impression" upon the president and himself, and that he had stated that Seymour "Could Succeed without the friends of Andrew Johnson, Chief Justice Chase, or Genl Hancock." Van Buren "is a very fine Gentleman but don't Suit that kind of business," Latham complained. Wood forwarded Latham's letter to presidential candidate Seymour.[96] At this point we leave the serpentine political trail briefly, but Latham, Stanton, Fernando Wood, and others of our characters will reappear as the Alaska scandal unfolds.

Chairman Banks was as confident as Latham when he shared his triumph with his beloved wife, but his hopes for reward ran in quite a different direction:

All my friends congratulate me on the Splendid vote we had yester-day. We had really 150 votes out of 201. Every body seems pleased. I forgot to say yesterday that the Chinese ambassadors were present during the debate and were much pleased. The Secretary of State was delighted. Every one tells me that I am to go to Russia. At a dinner it was the subject of conversation, & all agreed it was now the best mission in Europe, That is the most interesting & impor-tant. This was the opinion of your friend Mr [Edwin] Stanton the late Secretary of War. I am told the French mission has been very active against Alaska. The opposition included every leader of the Republican party in the House except Mr Stevens whose support had something of damage in it because he was so violent. All sides of the House give your Husband the credit of carrying, & it is regarded by the men who have longest acquaintance with Congress as a very remarkable triumph.[97]

The rejoicing of the Alaska men was abruptly cut short. The an-tipathy of many members of the House to the Johnson administra-tion and their distrust of the Senate's easy acquiescence to Alaska, which C.C. Washburn had deftly exploited, raised a threatening constitutional issue between the two chambers. The bill providing $7.2 million initiated by the House of Representatives included a preamble insisting that the assent of "Congress" was necessary on appropriations, cession of territory, and the rights of inhabitants *before* the treaty could take effect. At the request of Sumner's For-eign Relations Committee, the Senate without a dissenting vote stripped the preamble from the bill as an unwarranted and uncon-stitutional claim. The *New York Tribune* speculated hopefully that the Senate might let the appropriation go over until the new ses-sion in December, if it did not get its way.[98] Such a move would seriously endanger the purchase.

Banks asked the House not to concur in the Senate's action in removing the preamble. To maintain control over the delicate situa-tion, he had himself appointed one of three representatives to con-fer with the other house. A deadlock threatened briefly, until the congress agreed to a revised preamble. It contained a "whereas" clause to satisfy each chamber: "Whereas the President had entered into a treaty with the Emperor of Russia and the Senate thereafter gave its advice and consent to said treaty," and "whereas said stipula-tions cannot be carried into full force and effect, except by legisla-tion to which the consent of both Houses of Congress is necessary." Robert J. Walker again circulated on the floor of the House of Rep-resentatives while the compromise was effected. Banks, with one eye cocked cautiously on the Senate, disclaimed any intent to seek a role in *treaty-making* when he presented his colleagues with the new version; but he assured them that the rights of the House over *legislation* had been preserved. He cut off Butler's attempt to prolong the vigorous debate and easily mustered votes to defeat Elihu Washburne's request for reconsideration. On July 23, the appropriation finally carried, by a margin of 91 to 48 with a telltale 77 not voting. More than fifteen months had elapsed since the Senate's ratification of the Alaska treaty.[99]

The *New York Tribune*, reflecting the clear mandate of many leading newspapers for economy in government and restrictions on the expansionism of the Johnson administration and the Senate, drew good-humored solace from the outcome:

> . . . We believe President Johnson was guilty of a gross usurpation in taking possession of Mr. Seward's hard bargain before Congress had sanctioned the trade. And now, we trust the House will be held to have given fair notice that this assumption must not be repeated. We have the old verdict — "Not guilty; but mustn't do so again."
>
> Gentlemen who want to sell us Northern Mexico, Lower California, St. Thomas, St. John, Bay of Samana, and other knick-knacks! understand once for all, that both Houses of Congress must assent or there is no valid trade! We have debt enough and none too much gold; our Government costs enough, and ought not to be rendered more expensive, as every outlying possession surely *will* make it. Be content, please do, with this haul, and keep your hands henceforth out of our pockets![100]

Four days later, Greeley's organ ridiculed Seward's policies a final time:

> It is reported that the King of the Feejee Islands, who owes us $45,000 and cannot pay it, wants Mr. Seward to buy his entire possessions as a good and easy means of settling the pecuniary embarrassment. We are opposed to Government land speculations on principle; but really there is something particularly attractive in this little scheme, and we are half tempted to disregard our own advice and recommend Mr. Seward to make a trade. The property is worth a great deal more than Alaska.

The *Tribune* jibed that Seymour and Blair could be named governor and military governor.[101]

The remaining task, with the United States already in possession of Alaska, was to pay the Czar's representatives. Almost every major newspaper described the process in detail, perhaps because the nation was suffering from severe monetary stringency at the time. There were stories about the preparation of the warrants by Treasurer Francis Spinner, the signing of the draft for $7.2 million and its delivery to Stoeckl, his receipt, and the transfer to the assistant treasurer in New York City for payment by gold certificates.[102] No suspicion then appeared of wrongdoing in any of these steps, but each was to figure in the later scandal and congressional investigation. The Republican *Washington Evening Star* revealed only that Stoeckl delivered to President Johnson a letter of congratulations from the czar for escaping conviction on impeachment. The Russian envoy reportedly had received the letter some time earlier but carefully held it until the appropriation bill became law.[103]

Stoeckl meanwhile informed St. Petersburg that the "Perkins affair" had "involved expenditures that would absorb a large part of the $200,000 which were given to me on the eve of the signature to cover the secret expenses." He complained, too, of the tribulations he had been forced to bear over Alaska and urgently requested some months of rest. "Do not ask me to remain or give me a place elsewhere," he begged, but "let me have the means of breathing for a time an atmosphere purer than that of Washington." His government granted him leave with pay for four months. He confided to the secretary of state when he left the capital early in October that he would return only if Seward remained in office. Stoeckl never came back, for he resigned in early 1869 from the Russian diplomatic service. The emperor had complimented him generously, Stoeckl wrote his friend Seward from St. Petersburg some months later, and had given him "a very handsome remuneration." He planned to "travel and rest for one or two years," then reenter the emperor's service "if need be."[104]

Seward likewise began to look ahead to the prospect of travel upon retirement from public life. He desired to see the Far West, Asia, and, of course, Alaska. In the meantime, there was work to be done, possibly even the annexation of other territories. "It is not my fault," he told residents of his hometown, Auburn, New York, on October 31, 1868, if the American flag "is still jealously excluded by European nations from the ever verdant islands of the Caribbean sea."[105]

Robert J. Walker's first thought was to put his personal affairs in order. He exuberantly informed his generous friend, W.W. Corcoran, on August 7, that it was a "pleasure to comply" with his benefactor's request for repayment. George W. Riggs, Washington banker and Corcoran's former associate, had received the Alaska drafts on Stoeckl's behalf. Walker explained, "When the money was handed me by Mr. Riggs, I requested him to write and inform you of my good fortune. This he promised he or Mr. Hyde would do." His financial obligations relieved, Walker turned with relish to penning political and financial articles meant to help Seymour and Blair.[106]

Russian America had become American Alaska in deed, with public and private accounts seemingly settled. Most legislators and doubtless many citizens as well — whatever their views of Seward's arctic bargain — welcomed the presumed conclusion of the protracted, unpleasant, suspicion-tinged controversy. They expected Congress to block any other attempts at expansion.

The Alaska affair, however, was not at an end. Suspicions seared politics during the late summer of 1868, and hints of wrongdoing over Alaska reemerged among the rumors. Inquisitive newsmen, sometimes spurred by other issues and lured by false leads, published sweeping insinuations against prominent newspapers, lobbyists, and congressmen. Their stories eventually compelled the House of Representatives to investigate. Congressional inquiries then were primitive but often as harried and tendentious as in recent times. Congressmen then as now were adept, too, in shielding fellow members if they wished to do so. In this instance, they left key allegations unresolved while exonerating the guilty with the innocent. Yet, the process of the congressional investigation of the Alaska scandal and the results of the inquiry embarrassed accusers and accused alike, and unwittingly further tarnished expansion. Such was the aftermath of the acquisition of Alaska.

CHAPTER TWO

THE ALASKA SCANDAL

The late summer news from Alaska in 1868 was not of gold strikes. General Henry Halleck, an original enthusiast for the purchase, reported "a bad state of affairs" in the territory following his tour of military posts. The Indians and Eskimos were "dissatisfied and perplexed" because of the removal of the patriarchal Russian Fur Company. American traders and troopers held the natives responsible for taking care of themselves and instructed them "rather in the vices than the virtues of civilization." Courts-martial were not required immediately, Halleck advised, but changes must be made.[1]

Scandals affecting the natives in distant Alaska drew little notice in Washington. Stirring subjects for investigation existed closer at hand and caused a marked sensitivity to scandal in the capital. There had been rumors of "whisky frauds," for instance, ever since Congress placed an excise tax on distilled spirits during the Civil War. In 1864 the issue had exploded on the floor of the House when Representative Francis P. Blair angrily defended himself against aspersions in the press that he was a whisky speculator.[2] Early in 1868, a subcommittee of Ways and Means took testimony from revenue detectives who had been spying into alleged corruption. Prominent Illinois Republican Representative Norman Judd — wartime minister to Berlin and friend of Lincoln and Grant — made inquiries on his own designed to force further probes into the Internal Revenue Bureau's handling of whisky taxes and bonded warehouses.[3]

Stories of corruption abounded in the press by March 1868, just as the impeachment trial of President Johnson was to begin. Even Democratic organs such as the *Washington Daily National Intelligencer* carried reports that the President himself "stands like adamant to protect his friends" in the whisky frauds.[4] Senate Secretary John W. Forney, writing under the pseudonym "Occasional" for his *Philadelphia Press* and *Washington Chronicle*, complained of rampant dishonesty in government. Conviction of Johnson was the remedy:

> The unexampled frauds in the collection of the whiskey tax, which have corrupted and demoralized more men than a thousand old United States banks, each conducted by a more daring financier than Mr. Biddle, will be checked the moment impeachment is a fixed fact. The conflict between the President, Secretary [of the Treasury Hugh] McCulloch, and Commissioner [of Internal Revenue E. A.] Rollins, has practically defeated the honest operations of the internal revenue law, by making it a gigantic instrument in the hands of reckless Copperhead politicians. Andrew Johnson is the ready and convenient shield for this unsurpassed profligacy. Mr. Rollins reports the offenders to the Secretary, and if they happen to be favorites of the Executive, Secretary McCulloch is directed to retain them. I have heard more than one honest officer in this service declare that the resulting frauds have become so stupendous and incessant that it is almost impossible to execute the law. . . . Needy politicians are enriched, and large funds amassed for use in the elections against the Republicans. . . . Millions of dollars have been returned, in defiance of law, to rebel cotton speculators and railroad companies; and these have been employed (doubtless by a previous understanding) without stint or concealment against the acts of reconstruction. . . . Although there are some honest men in that department of the Government, the mere fact that it is crowded with active sympathizers with treason . . . under the guise of "special agents" shows at a glance what a dangerous engine it has become.[5]

Similar allegations of corruption became entangled with the impeachment trial. After the impeachment managers failed to convict President Johnson with their first and strongest charge, they opened hearings into allegations that the "Whisky Ring" had bribed senators to vote for acquittal. Representative Ben Butler, who was himself accused of offering payment for votes to convict, believed that Johnson's supporters had bribed four senators. It was alleged that well-known Cincinnati gambler Charles W. Woolley, New York Internal Revenue Collector Sheridan Shook, and others had employed $20,000 to $25,000 on behalf of Johnson. Shook denied the accusation, but one witness testified that Republican Senator Samuel Pomeroy of Kansas had offered his own vote and that of others to the President for $40,000.[6] The press reported various details of these stories, which became popular currency.

The House report of the impeachment investigation, which was printed on July 3, in the midst of the Alaska debate and on the eve of the Democratic convention, traced the money to another source.

It charged that a fund for Johnson's defense had been collected in the New York Customs House, that $22,000 had been used to secure the election of the "recusant" Senator Edmund Ross of Kansas, and that Johnson had known as early as March 30 that seven senators would vote for his acquittal.[7] Late in July, Ben Butler sharply criticized Democratic Senator John Henderson of Missouri for having talked with the President's private secretary and other agents during the impeachment trial. The *New York Times*, among other papers, printed an incriminating letter from the secretary to Johnson about contacts with Henderson: "Dear Mr. President: The Henderson matter all right. Lacy has been to see him with Craig. All right! So says Evarts. Cooper."[8]

Odors of still another scandal arose at this time, fanned by the furor of the impeachment proceedings and wafting redolent for months.[9] This was the Alta Vela affair. Alta Vela, an islet fifteen miles south of Santo Domingo, contained deposits of guano, a valued fertilizer in the mid-nineteenth century. Agents of the Baltimore firm of Patterson and Murguiendo had found the deposits in 1860 and taken possession of the little island. They filed claim of ownership with the Department of State, as a law of 1856 required, before commencing to extract the guano. Soon thereafter, Spain "reannexed" the Dominican Republic. Spanish officials, learning of the guano discovery, not only claimed the nearby islet and expelled the Baltimore firm but sold the rights to the New York company of Root, Webster, and Clark.

Patterson and Murguiendo complained to Secretary of State Jeremiah Black of the Buchanan administration and later hired that distinguished Democratic lawyer and his son as counsels. Black's successor as secretary of state, Seward, ignored the claimants' demands in 1861 for firm action and, in 1867, for the dispatch of a warship to Alta Vela. Seward did not want to disturb relations with Spain, which were tolerably good during the Civil War, while he faced serious problems with England and France. After Appomattox, his desire to obtain Samaná Bay from the newly independent Dominican Republic for use as a naval base precluded pressing the issue of Alta Vela. Besides, the State Department's claim examiner questioned the Baltimore firm's rights, and Black himself had ruled negatively in 1859 on a similar guano case. Patterson and Murguiendo supposed that the reason for Seward's refusal was his friendship with Thurlow Weed, whom they believed was interested in the New York firm. Judge Black and his associate, Colonel J.W. Shaffer, responded vigorously to Seward's stand in petitions of July and August 1867 and in visits with the President. Their financial stake increased on March 3, 1868, when the Baltimore firm pledged Black a percentage of the profits.[10]

Lawyer-client relations simultaneously became snarled because Johnson ignored Seward's advice not to employ Black and by March 7 engaged his friend as one of his defense counsels in the impeachment case. He stubbornly insisted that Black knew his negative views on Alta Vela. Unfortunately for all concerned, Black and his partners meant to persuade the President to change his mind on the guano case.

Associate counsel Shaffer, urged on by the Baltimore claimants, also sought support from members of Congress. This move hopelessly entangled Alta Vela with the impeachment trial. Shaffer, who had once served as aide-de-camp to General Butler, persuaded the Massachusetts Republican to draft a letter to the President endorsing the need for "forcible" action on behalf of the Alta Vela claimants. Butler not only took this extraordinary step, he secured endorsements for the plea on March 9 from six other Republican representatives. Three of the signers were fellow impeachment managers — Stevens, John A. Logan of Illinois, and John A. Bingham of Ohio — while a fourth, William H. Koontz of Pennsylvania, was to be a witness against Johnson. Butler insisted that he had prepared the draft letter in February before impeachment was determined, but the managers' poor judgment was manifest.[11]

Johnson, given the letter by Black's son on March 10, instantly suspected the petitioners of seeking to make a profit of a half million or million dollars each. He also interpreted the letter as a proposal that he purchase his acquittal by recognizing the claim. Black, meanwhile, threatened to quit as counsel on the eve of the Senate trial unless the President abandoned Seward on the Alta Vela issue. Johnson typically refused to retreat under pressure, and Black withdrew from the case on March 19 after failing to budge the President. Black complained sourly that "Mr. Seward's little finger" was "thicker than the loins of the law," while Johnson waxed indignant about the judge's behavior.[12]

The contretemps, which inevitably seeped into the press, was not yet at an end. Colonel Shaffer stated publicly that correspondence in the files of the Department of State demonstrated Weed's involvement. He carefully avoided repeating this accusation in a legal paper sent to Johnson, but Black compounded the insult by describing Weed as one of Seward's "thieving friends." Another of the President's lawyers, rough and ready T.A.R. Nelson, introduced the affair into the Senate trial on April 24. Nelson, a former Tennessee representative, obviously was attempting to impugn the impeachment managers. He spoke of an extensive speculation, though he did not implicate the managers, and charged explicitly that the petitions on Alta Vela "were all gotten up after this impeachment proceeding was commenced."[13]

Ben Butler and Nelson engaged in a nasty quarrel four days later over the counsel's remarks. Thad Stevens stubbornly insisted on the House floor that the petition had been shown to Johnson without his authorization. He had nothing to retract, he stormed, for the document expressed his known position on such issues. Thurlow Weed indignantly cried slander and asserted that he knew nothing whatever of Alta Vela. Weed had been involved in the sale of the guano properties, but both Seward's report to the President and subsequent research generally attest to his innocence in this instance. He characteristically lashed back. The old Whig editor exposed Black's financial interest in the claim and unfairly accused him of expecting to profit from the removal of Johnson and Seward.[14] The entire complicated affair, which received particular prominence in the *New York Herald*, interrupted the impeachment proceedings, tore raw political nerves, and sharpened popular suspicions of rottenness in government.

As always, the press did not immediately disclose every fraud that it uncovered, but insiders circulated the stories privately. John Russell Young, the youthful managing editor of the *New York Tribune*, discovered corruption ultimately to dwarf the Alta Vela affair. Young revealed what he had unearthed in a letter of July 17, 1868, to Elihu Washburne, the statesmanlike Illinois representative, who enjoyed virtually exclusive political access to General Grant during the presidential campaign.

> I have been looking into this Pacific Railroad business, as it appears in the case of an injunction asked for by a New York party, and find an almost incredible amount of corruption connected with it, — especially the Credit Mobilier — affecting a good many members of Congress, the names of whom astonish me. I should like to open

broadsides on the whole thing, but the danger is in doing so now we throw a scandal upon the party and affect the next election. This is the only thing that makes me hesitate, and I do not know as that will last.

The skies are bright for Grant and Colfax; but we must do our best work to elect them.

One thing more should be done, Young urged: "Cannot you by some means convince Congress to leave Washington and go home?"[15]

The corruption of Credit Mobilier, the construction company of the government-subsidized Union Pacific Railroad, popularly is associated with the Grant administration or is known as the dramatic revelation of 1872. The fraud had occurred well before the first election of Grant, however, and newspapermen such as John Russell Young knew about it in mid-1868.

The smell of corruption was in the air in July 1868. Uriah Painter, correspondent for the *Philadelphia Inquirer* and *New York Sun*, sensed something amiss in the Alaska appropriation and meant to expose the swindle. A confidant of Alaska's congressional opponents, Painter had told them of Seward's designs on Greenland and Iceland before publishing the story in the *Sun* on July 1. The reporter knew as well that Robert J. Walker was the author of the *Chronicle* articles; he also had seen Governor Walker seated prominently at the Democratic convention and observed him in the House chamber during the protracted debates on Alaska. But Walker enjoyed the right of the House floor because he was a former member of the Senate, so Painter needed more incriminating information about his lobbying for the appropriation bill.

Tipped off that Frederick P. Stanton was working with Walker, Painter approached Stanton in the corridor of the Capitol at the time of the House debates. Painter later reconstructed their conversation, for the House investigating committee:

> "I understand you are engaged in this Alaska matter." He [Stanton] replied, "No, sir; I have nothing at all to do with it." I remarked, "I was told this morning by a man that you were in it; and now," said I, "this thing is all wrong, and you will get blown higher than you anticipate, if you do not let the thing alone;" and he declared to me, upon his honor, that he had not anything at all to do with it. . . .
>
> I said: "Are you not still a partner of Mr. Walker?" He replied that he was in some things. I then asked him if Walker was not in it. He said he did not know. I said I guessed he was, and told him

the first time he met Walker to put it right to him and see if he would not acknowledge it. I thought it was a big swindle. . . . I met him subsequently and I think he told me that he had asked Mr. Walker, but he totally disabused my mind of the fact that Walker had anything to do with it. He completely disarmed me of my suspicion by his apparent frankness and explicitness.[16]

Painter, contrary to his testimony, remained suspicious, but so far he had failed to learn Stanton's secrets. Near the end of the debate in July he twice mentioned in his stories the presence of Walker on the House floor, although he carefully drew no conclusions. Meanwhile, he sought information from Stanton's associate Robert Latham, whom Painter had known intimately for about ten years:

I said to him one day: "Are you in this Alaska business?" He said no; that he did not know anything about it. I asked him if Stanton or Walker were in it, and he replied that he guessed not. Says I, "When you see Stanton go right at him and ask him if there is money in it or not." He told me subsequently that he had asked Stanton and he denied it.[17]

Painter was on the right track but erred in underestimating the slyness of Stanton and Latham and in not realizing that they were as much a target for investigation as the more prestigious Walker.

It must be mentioned here that Stanton gave House investigators a very different account of his conversation with Painter, whom he accused of soliciting money to influence congressional votes and of threatening to oppose the bill when he did not get it.[18] Governor Walker, one of the most persuasive men in Washington, told a like story to the House investigating committee.[19] Walker had never met Painter, however, and repeated only what he had heard from Stanton, who had no reason to portray the reporter's inquiries in a friendly manner.

Painter may actually have suggested to Stanton in July 1868 that he be employed to lobby for Alaska. In all likelihood, his motive was to lead Stanton on, rather than to join the lobby. He had a reputation for being an "industrious reporter" who would "play possum" and "do almost anything" to get a story.[20] Painter tried repeatedly in July 1868 to ferret out the lobby.[21] He succeeded only in angering Walker and placing Stanton and Latham on their guard. He learned nothing of substance.

Then, a few weeks later, a curious passage occurred. The incident revived all of Painter's suspicions and led him — and some subse-

quent scholars — onward and astray. On August 18, 1868, Robert
J. Walker was robbed of $16,000 in gold certificates while riding
on the Greene Street railroad car in New York City. He was the
prey of a female pickpocket, who found her diminutive victim an
easy mark. His waistcoat typically askew and bulging with papers,
Walker did not discover his loss until the thief left the streetcar. He
at once notified police, who sent out bulletins and announced a
reward. The newspapers were not informed until nine days later,
when it was revealed that Buffalo authorities had arrested three
men. The suspects, immediately identified as well-known New York
thieves, had been trying to sell a $1,000 gold certificate. A New
York City detective sent to Buffalo quickly recovered two of the
missing $5,000 certificates and expected shortly to find the third.
Two of the three prisoners were transported back to New York City
for arraignment at Jefferson Market Police Court. Walker declined
to prosecute them, and they were released.[22]

The current columns of New York's newspapers contained many
similar tidings of thefts and arrests. This case attracted somewhat
more attention because the victim was former Secretary of the
Treasury Robert J. Walker and because the money stolen — though
not larger in amount than in several other crimes of the day —
consisted of gold certificates. The efficiency of the police also drew
notice. The sensation-minded *New York Herald*, which carried a
lengthy account, trumpeted that this was "A Police Case With a
Mystery," in which all the facts were not known even though the
crime had been solved. The *Times* and the *World* merely headlined
and described the theft, arrest, and recovery. The *Washington Daily
Morning Chronicle* featured "The Walker Bond Robbery," though
the story referred accurately to certificates and not to bonds.[23]
Curiously, the *New York Sun* did not carry a report.

The *Sun's* Uriah Painter, who happened to be in the city, read
the story in another newspaper. He agreed that this was indeed a
mysterious case. He also sensed the solution: Robert J. Walker was
in New York City to pay the bribes promised congressmen by the
Alaska lobby. Painter, according to his later testimony, confronted
Latham when he returned to Washington: "You see Walker has lost
his checks, and this thing is going to be investigated, and you will
find that your friend Stanton is in it." He charged Latham with
being in it, too.[24] Painter also broke the news to Stanton, asking
him "what he supposed Mr. Walker was using these $5,000 gold

checks about, and if he did not think it was some of the Alaska money held by him. He said he did not know."[25]

Stanton, in his subsequent testimony on this point, recalled the conversation in more revealing detail:

> . . . I met Mr. Painter again on Fourteenth street, near the office of the Philadelphia Inquirer. He stopped me and said, "I saw[,] Mr. Stanton[,] that Governor Walker had been robbed in New York of some gold certificates, of $5,000 each. He had just got his money split up into $5,000 certificates, and was going to the Fifth Avenue Hotel to distribute it." Said I, "to whom?" Well, he intimated (I do not remember whether he said it in direct terms or not) that it was to members of Congress. I said to Mr. Painter that I knew he was mistaken in that particular; that Governor Walker had received something upwards of $20,000, but that I was very sure he had not paid any of it away to members of Congress. He replied that he knew better; that he had ascertained that only $5,000,000 of that money had gone to the Russian government, and that the other $2,000,000 and upwards had been disposed of here for the passage of that bill. I told him I did not know anything about that, but that I did not believe it. He said that he intended, at any rate, to have an investigation.[26]

One historian who tried to unravel the strands of this affair conjectured that the reason Walker declined to prosecute the men arrested was to avoid publicity. If so, the scheme backfired badly. Another historian came closer to the mark when he wrote that "this strange tale was naturally another basis for the rumors of distribution of money," adding that the House investigating committee curiously asked no questions of Walker about it.[27] The House inquiry slighted the robbery as it did more important matters. But the Greene Street affair really deserved little congressional attention, although it was the inspiration for new rumors. Painter himself invented and circulated the most incriminating of them, the alleged plan for a payoff in New York City.

His suppositions can be set aside. It is unlikely that any congressmen were waiting at the elegant Fifth Avenue Hotel for Walker to reward them. None had registered there on Tuesday, August 18, or in the preceding few days, so far as can be determined.[28] Democratic Representative J.V.L. Pruyn of New York, veteran regent of the University of the State of New York who was retiring from Congress to become chancellor of the University, checked in at the hotel the next day. He was an improbable accomplice and he had abstained from voting on the Alaska appropriation.[29]

All the gold certificates, moreover, could easily be identified. Only the $1,000 certificate was negotiable—Walker immediately stopped payment on it—while the three $5,000 certificates were non-negotiable. The hoodlums who obtained the certificates had not been able to dispose of them, and at least two newspapers remarked at the time that the larger certificates could not be transferred. Walker would have required different currency had he been on his way to pay off bribes or debts.[30]

These troublesome facts did not deter Painter, who energetically resumed his investigation. He knew now from what Stanton revealed that Walker had obtained $20,000 from the Russian government but incorrectly believed that the money was meant to bribe congressmen. Certain that the robbery revealed only the tip of the Alaska iceberg, he pursued still another lead—wholly false—which ironically drew him and the whole affair closer to disclosure.

He stumbled upon the clue in a newspaper article. Painter read in a cable dispatch that $5 million in gold had been sent to Russia through London. This meant to him that $2.2 million from the Alaska purchase had been used along the way for bribery, as he implied to Stanton in their last conversation.[31] There is, of course, a law of newspaper reports: for every revelation there comes in time a correction, which gets less notice. In this case, the *New York Times* explained four months later that the remittance from London of $5 million (a million pounds sterling) involved Russian railroad negotiations, not Alaska.[32]

Uriah Painter was on the trail of the "missing" $2.2 million well before the *Times* issued its correction. Sometime in the autumn he interviewed General Francis Spinner, the treasurer of the United States. He learned that Washington banker George W. Riggs had not received the money at once but drew it out gradually in checks of various sizes from August 1 to September 16. Spinner verified later that there had been six transfer checks and that Riggs had left $100,000 on special deposit after August 1:[33]

Transfer check #3031	$7,000,000	August 1
3032	100,000	August 1
3036	25,000	August 3
3037	35,000	August 4
3120	20,000	September 9
3146	20,000	September 16

Painter asserted in his subsequent testimony that Spinner also revealed to him another peculiar aspect of the transaction. The story that Spinner allegedly had disclosed was that Riggs had asked, on "the day that the papers were signed, after the money was appropriated," for a loan of $200,000 in greenbacks at once on security of the gold. Secretary of the Treasury McCulloch had referred the matter to Spinner, saying that the money was wanted at once since Congress had just adjourned. Painter said that Spinner saw no reason why this sum could not be furnished as a courtesy to the Russians, since no risk was involved.[34]

Spinner disagreed with Painter's statement in important details and supported his version with records and cancelled drafts. The treasurer testified that "someone" had come to him on August 1 and asked about such a transaction, that he had considered the idea "safe," but that no action was taken. Banker Riggs denied that he ever asked for a loan of greenbacks.

What may have happened is that Spinner originally did not make himself clear or exaggerated the incident to Painter. It is also possible that Painter himself misunderstood Spinner and made too much of what he had heard. The reporter was quick to draw extreme conclusions because a figure of $200,000 would help to account for part of the $2.2 million that he mistakenly thought had not been sent to Russia. Painter also believed that Stoeckl's payoffs had to come out of the $7.2 million. It is clear that Walker's large retainer and other payments did come from the appropriation made by Congress, but Stoeckl, as mentioned earlier, also had been given $200,000 "on the eve of the signature" to deal with the Perkins claim. He reported spending this money to forestall the claim. (He did not buy off the claimants, for they were unrelenting.) Undoubtedly, with the expensive help of Stanton and Latham, he used some of it to bribe reporters and otherwise promote the treaty. He probably lined his own pockets as well.

Painter, however, did not know of the Russian money and believed it was the appropriation — American money — that had been used corruptly. He indignantly confronted Stanton again. Painter blurted that Riggs was putting out the money "in sums of about $30,000 each," including one payment to the wife of a congressman from Ohio. The "damned rascals" lied to him, he complained, and had distributed large bribes. Stanton, as before, revealed nothing to the reporter.[35] Painter therefore did not obtain the information he needed for a story.

Investigative reporter Uriah Painter was not alone in reflecting during the late summer of 1868 on the uses made of the $7.2 million paid for Alaska. President Andrew Johnson formulated his own version of the Alaska scandal. The President considered the tale he heard important enough so that he wrote it down in a memorandum, an unusual act for him:

> On the 6th Sept Sundy 1868 Mr. Seward and myself rode out some seven or eight miles on the Road leading to Malsboro Md — near place called old fields, we drove out into a shady grove of oak trees — while there taking some refreshment, in the current of conversation on various subjects, the Secretary asked the question if it had ever occurred to me how few members there were in congress whose actions were entirely above and beyond pecuniary influence. I replied that I had never attempted to reduce it to an accurate calculation, but regretted to confess that there was a much smaller number exempt than at one period of life I had supposed them to be — He then stated you remember that the appropriation of the seven $ million for the payment of Alaska to the Russia Govnt was hung up or brought to a dead lock in the H of Reps — While the appropriation was thus delayed the Russian minister stated to me that John W. Forney stated to him that he needed $30,000 that he had lost $40,000, by a faithless friend and that he wanted the $30,000 in gold — That there was no chance of the appropriation passing the House of Reps without certain influence was brought to bear in its favor — The 30,000 was paid hence the advocacy of the appropriation in the Chronicle — He also stated that $20,000 was paid to R.J. Walker and F.P. Stanton for their services — N P Banks chairman of the committee on foreign relations $8000, and that the incoruptable Thaddeous Stevens received as his 'sop' the moderate sum of $10,000 — All these sums were paid by the Russian minister directly and indirectly to the respective parties to secure appropriation of money the Govnt had stiputed to pay the Russian Govnt in solemn treaty which had been ratified by both Govmts. —
>
> Banks and Stevens was understood to be the counsel for a claim against the Russian Govnt for Arms which had been furnished by some of our citizens — known as the Perkins Claim — Hence a fee for their influence in favor of the appropriation &c — Banks was chairman of the Committee on foreign retions — [36]

Seward was an ingratiating and effusive man, especially on a social occasion with those he wished to impress. Johnson certainly relished learning that his mortal enemies Forney and "the incoruptable Thaddeous Stevens" had taken bribes. But the President, who was known to enjoy "refreshments," might not have heard or recorded the telling conversation precisely.

Some of the allegations are unconvincing on their face. Seward's remark about the need for influence to secure the appropriation conflicts with every other account and with his own earlier expressions of confidence about passage of the bill. And Simon Stevens, not Thaddeus, served as counsel for the Perkins claim. It also seems unlikely that the elderly Stevens needed to have been bribed. He did at first champion the Perkins claim but he shifted after Seward and Stoeckl talked with him in the late spring and never subsequently held the claim against the appropriation. Stoeckl might have bought his support during his visit, or Robert Walker could have done it during a meeting in mid-July. But this seems unlikely, for Stevens was a consistent advocate of the acquisition of Alaska from the signing of the treaty to the passage of the appropriation bill. Moreover, Old Thad, whose life had been sustained by his hatred of the President and by the hope that Johnson might still be removed from office, had been ill since before Congress adjourned in July; he died on August 11.

Johnson's improbable tale holds something more, however, both for those interested in mysteries and for those concerned with morals in government. Seward's conversation with Johnson occurred several days *before* banker Riggs withdrew the last $40,000 from the Treasury. The remaining $40,000, therefore, could not have been employed in any payoff to this time. But it could have been used subsequently. A second arresting fact is that the President and secretary of state possessed information that a foreign if friendly government allegedly had paid money to two United States officials, Representatives Banks and Stevens. Not for another hundred years did withholding information constitute the obstruction of justice, but Johnson and Seward should have revealed what they knew to Congress.

The secretary of state was telling tales again two weeks after his private picnic with the President. On September 23, Seward entertained the distinguished diplomat and editor John Bigelow at his home. After dinner the two men went into an adjacent parlor for a game of whist, in which Edouard Stoeckl shortly was to join them. They stopped to admire Leutze's impressive painting of the signing of the Alaska treaty, and then the irrepressible Seward asked Bigelow:

> "Do you wish to know how that treaty was consummated?" I said "Yes." "Then I must put you under Oath. Before that money could be voted $20,000 had to be given to R.J. Walker $10,000 to his part-

ner F. K. Stanton $10,000 to ten members of Congress — & $20,000 to Forney who had lost $40,000 by the defalcation of his clerk. $10,000 more were to be given to poor Thad Stevens but no one would undertake to give that to him so I undertook it [my]self. The poor fellow died and I have it now."

Bigelow recorded Seward's revelations in his diary.[37]

There are, as historian David Hunter Miller pointed out, intriguing similarities and differences in names as well as amounts between Johnson's memorandum and Bigelow's diary account of what Seward disclosed. Forney, Walker, and Stanton appear in both versions, Banks only in Johnson's. Bigelow added ten unnamed congressmen, reduced Forney's reward by $10,000, and gave Stanton his own $10,000. He also left Stevens's $10,000 with Seward. He did not directly implicate Stoeckl, with whom he shortly shuffled cards, and made no mention of the Perkins claim as Johnson had done.[38]

What is to be made of all this? Walker and Stanton did obtain Russian money, though neither Johnson nor Bigelow got the sums quite right. Seward's confession that he possessed the money meant for Stevens can hardly be denied if it were certain that Bigelow was an accurate scribe. Other details of the two discrepant versions require some verification before they can be entirely credited. The secretary certainly twice talked of Russian payments, once just before and once shortly after Riggs withdrew the last $40,000 from the Treasury. But Johnson and Bigelow apparently were discreet about what the secretary told them. No more was heard of Seward's tales until historians uncovered them forty years and more later. As will be seen, his revelations — even the references to Walker — did not inspire or figure in the subsequent congressional inquiry.

Whatever secrets Stoeckl revealed to his friend Seward, there is no doubt that the Russian minister disbursed some of the moneys at his disposal — at least $200,000 — to Walker, Stanton, Latham, Forney, and other newspapermen. In all likelihood, he also rewarded the adept legation secretary, Bodisco, who had participated actively in the lobbying and remained in Washington when Stoeckl left the United States. There are reasons to think that Stoeckl obtained a larger portion for himself. He had been sorely disappointed by what he considered the emperor's meager compensation for his outstanding services in negotiating the treaty, and now he could secure his just reward. He would never be called to account in the United States. Three weeks after he played whist with Seward and

Bigelow, he stole away from Washington forever. He had long intended to leave America, but his escape at this time gave him even
more satisfaction. Seven months later, he wrote to Seward that the
emperor "regreted (sic) my leaving Washington" but had given him
"a very handsome remuneration." He explained that he would travel
and rest for a year or two and then "reinter (sic) the service, if need
be."[39] Alaska had caused him endless troubles, but Stoeckl at last
had made it the source of his fortune. The fact that the money could
be considered American must have eased his conscience and afforded
him additional pleasure.

Alaska, too, slipped from attention. Political interest centered
on the presidential campaign, although the outcome was certain.
Democratic organizers attempted to stir fears in the northeastern
states by circulating pictures of the black Mississippi legislature, but
several leading Democratic newspapers abandoned hope for Seymour and Blair and called for a new ticket.

The political maneuvering behind the scenes was crude and opportunistic. One incident illustrates the tone of the contest. Republican national secretary William E. Chandler, who wrote Elihu
Washburne that this was "the time to smash the Democratic party
in pieces if possible," revealed that he had an opportunity "to in-
vest in the *Intelligencer*." That paper was the sole remaining important Democratic organ in Washington. Chandler had discussed
the idea with Republican leaders and fund-raisers Horace Greeley,
Alexander Stewart, Edwin D. Morgan, General Daniel Sickles, and
Judge Edwards Pierrepont. He recognized the need for caution, since
the paper's proprietors were "a mercenary, unprincipled set. . . .
I may be mistaken in dickering with these scoundrels. 'Can a man
touch pitch and not be defiled?' — but I am conscious of the cor-
rectness and purity of my own motives."[40] The underhanded deal
finally fell through, and the *National Intelligencer* remained in its
party's ranks.[41] Grant easily triumphed over the stumbling Democracy, without the purchased endorsement of his opponents' opportunistic organ.

During the campaign, Uriah Painter busied himself on behalf
of the Republican candidates. After the election he picked up the
threads of his Alaska story. Other reports were circulating as well.
In one such story, Banks — and sometimes Seward — received
$250,000, while large sums went to General Butler and to a promi-
nent Democratic representative, Samuel Randall of Philadelphia.

The man carrying this canard around Washington's press rooms was a Colonel Robert Martin of Georgia. Painter did not know him, but he credited the story at first. He soon had second thoughts, perhaps because Martin also was circulating another story — one that Washington reporters had been hearing for some weeks. Martin alleged that the Alaska lobby had bought members of the press corps and several newspapers.[42]

Some correspondents, including R.J. Hinton of the *Worcester* (Mass.) *Daily Spy* and the lobbyist-reporters W.B. Shaw and E.P. Brooks, thought there was a foundation for Martin's reports.[43] Painter, however, did not credit them. Convinced that he knew the real story of the scandal, which he meant to publish, he wrote to Ben Butler on November 27 in order to obtain an investigation. He considered Butler, who was in Massachusetts until Congress reconvened on December 7, an enemy of the purchase and of corruption. Painter informed Butler of the three "facts" that he had unearthed: only $5 million went to Russia; Riggs had borrowed $200,000 in greenbacks; and Walker received $20,000. But he also took a swipe at unpopular Secretary of the Treasury McCulloch:

> I have in my possesion [sic] some facts in connection with the corruption by which the Treasury was robbed of the $7,200,000 to pay for the Alaska & if you desire will show how to uncover the biggest lobby swindle ever "put up" in Washington. The men who got the huge slices are in great trepidation at the leaking out of the fact that only $5,000,000 went to Russia. *Sec'y McCulloch* is somewhat disgusted because after loaning Riggs $200,000 in currency to make some of his payments for ~~Bodisco~~ the Baron, He did not get a "thank you sir"- "Little Bobby Walker" who wrote against & worked against impeachment & ran the Chase movement — got $20,000 — gold — When will you be here?
>
> I take it for granted you will come now, since the enemy here failed to defeat, or kill you.

Butler replied a week later with his customary brevity: "My dear Painter Will be there on Monday Yours BFB."[44]

Painter, who was anxious to scoop other correspondents, broke his story in the *Sun* on November 30, before Butler responded. It was the account he had been working on for weeks. Painter first alluded to the rumors of corruption that had circulated for months and to the cable announcement that only one million pounds sterling went to Russia. He asserted sarcastically that "disinterested par-

ties" who had trumpteted Alaska's virtues had divided "over two
hundred thousand dollars" when the money was drawn from the
Treasury. Greenbacks were borrowed on the gold, moreover, for
a further profit of "over 40 percent." Much of the money "was confiscated by middle men," Painter argued, and never reached the
intended parties. "One old gentleman of some distinction, who sat
upon the platform of Tammany Hall when Seymour was nominated,
was put in to the extent of $20,000 in gold, yet it is doubtful if he
really influenced the vote of a single member of the House. When
Congress meets the whole question will doubtless be investigated."[45]

The *Sun's* editor discounted his own reporter's allegations as a
"vague and general" contribution to the existing "very extensive
structure of rumor." Describing briefly the two prevalent versions —
that Russia received only $5 million, or that the lobbyists disbursed
merely $200,000 and got for themselves just the difference between
gold and greenbacks — the editor declared that the whole "highly
improbable" tale "ought not to be entertained for a moment without
better evidence." Dana ridiculed the idea that the Russian government would allow Stoeckl "to dabble in such dirty water" or that
Seward would have become involved, and he stressed the denial
by the *Sun* and the *Tribune* that either paper had received ten thousand dollars as sometimes alleged. "The other statement, that a
prominent politician who sometimes gets drunk has confessed to
having had twenty thousand dollars of this money, is equally un-
satisfactory." Not every baseless report deserves investigation, the
Sun concluded. Yet, the size of the Alaska transaction and the
eminence of the men involved made it proper to "examine the imputation and how utterly unsubstantial is the ground on which it
has been promulgated."[46]

On December 7, as Congress reconvened, the *Sun's* editor commented upon a brief story in the *Tribune* recalling, in part inaccurately, that in August Walker had "been robbed of $7,000 [*sic*] in
gold." Dana pondered this account of the summertime robbery and
the *Tribune's* implication that it was connected with the Alaska
affair, but he declined to believe this "entirely new feature of the
business." and questioned whether the *Tribune* had even "correctly
reported" the facts. He then turned to "the more ordinary rumor"
that "the alleged corruption money was paid in greenbacks, and
not gold" and that Walker had been paid "twenty thousand dollars." In offering this version Dana forgot that Painter's story about

clever greenback transactions also stated that Walker had been paid in gold, not in greenbacks. Countless similar errors, as well as intentional distortions, appeared in the press of the time. The variety of accounts compounded suspicions. Dana himself now conceded that, although "the *Tribune*'s report is marked with improbability, it is nonetheless the duty of Congress to investigate the whole subject . . . and put an end to all these disagreeable rumors." The next day, Painter reported from Washington that C.C. Washburn was looking into the Alaska lobby and that an investigation was likely.[47]

Another Alaska story on December 7 temporarily eclipsed the *Sun*'s clouded revelations. A lengthy report in the *Worcester* (Mass.) *Daily Spy* attracted notice throughout the country and caused an explosion on Capitol Hill. Correspondent R.J. Hinton, who signed the article with his penname "Observer," compiled all the Alaska gossip and a few references to the Whisky Ring as well. It is scarcely possible to imagine a greater hodgepodge of rumor and allegation. "Observer" himself carefully insisted that he was only reporting the stories being circulated, and he drew the basic framework for his story from Painter's reports. He identified a number of newspapers and Washington reporters as possible conspirators, however, in addition to naming banker Riggs and Walker as supposed profiteers. He concluded by suggesting an official investigation. The fact that the *Spy*'s owner, John D. Baldwin, was a Republican member of the House of Representatives added authenticity and drew attention. Many editors and other readers believed that Baldwin himself had written the article, but this view was mistaken. Nor was it true that Baldwin had any political interest in the piece. He was closer politically to Banks than to Butler within the Massachusetts delegation and had voted for the Alaska appropriation. He had not sought reelection in 1868 and would shortly leave Congress.[48]

After congratulating himself for being passed by in "all the schemes and jobs with which newspaper men are so often connected in this city," Hinton gave "the substance of rumors now afloat." It also was claimed, he said, "that checks, letters and affidavits will be forthcoming, if Congress shall order an investigation:"

> Of the $7,200,000 in gold voted for Alaska, the amount, it is now reported, Russia actually got was $5,000,000 in gold — about one million pounds sterling. This leaves $2,200,000 to be accounted for. How much of this went to pay for the collection, preparation, and publication of documents and reports of a favorable character, published

in all sorts of ways and by all sorts of persons, is more than can ever be guessed — doubtless a good round sum.

But with regard to the outside ring — the third house — the press, editors, and correspondents — it is reported that above $300,000 in greenbacks was spent among them. Mr. Riggs, a banker here, is said to have obtained from the Secretary of the Treasury, just at the close of the debates, etc., which terminated by the purchase of Alaska, a loan of the amount just specified. That loan was (if it had any real existence) for obvious reasons, never made public. Immediately on the receipt by Mr. Riggs, newspaper men and others known as lobbyists, were the owners of drafts of various amounts on the Treasurer of the United States, which it is declared Gen. Spinner's books will show were cashed.

A list of persons who are stated to have been thus paid has been circulating here for some time past. It certainly includes the names of persons to whom such a statement is a decided matter of surprise.

Among the sums specified in these reports are such items as New York Tribune, $20,000; manager of its Washington Bureau, $5,000; publisher of Washington Chronicle, $25,000. The correspondents of the Times, World, Boston Journal, Philadelphia Press, Chicago Tribune, Boston Advertiser, Evening Post, and others are all set down as having been paid various sums each, from $2,500 upward. Some of them are anxiously inquiring what has become of the money, as it has never been paid to them.

By the way, I find the belief is quite general among well-informed journalists here, that money was really paid out to some parties who represented their ability to influence the correspondents and journals aforesaid, but who played a shrewder game by trusting to the drift of discussion and events to bring opponents round to the measure, and keeping the money paid to themselves. The daughters of a member from Ohio got $10,000 each, but this, it is affirmed, was immediately sent back. An incident of a similar honorable character, told of the same gentleman, is very generally believed. In this case it was the whiskey ring that wanted to influence the important voice, and $10,000 was forwarded to one of his daughters. It was sent back immediately. To return to Alaska, however, Robert J. Walker got $25,000 in gold. The certificates for this amount were, I believe, stolen from him in Boston or New York. He makes no secret of his having received a large sum, but says it was a professional retainer from the Russian government. He appears also to have been acting professionally for his own government, as some part of the Riggs $300,000 appears to have passed into his hands. These are some of the rumors afloat, and the persons whose names are identified with them.

Now comes another chapter, to which it is declared the threatened expose is due. As before stated the $300,000 referred to was in greenbacks. The lobbyists, etc., were paid therein, they having been urgent for such payment as soon as the Alaska bill passed. But it is now reported that Mr. Riggs received from the "high contracting parties" this amount in gold, with which he paid back to the Treasury Mr. McCulloch's loan and netted to himself the nice little per cent, of $70,000, being the difference of 35 per cent between gold and legal tender. This commission is said to be outside of what he was paid for services rendered. The "harpies," vexed at being sold, are now talking about the matter. Some say the difference has been, or is to be, divided among the clamorous in order to hush matters up. Among other transactions, it is declared that the "Perkins claim," which at one time threatened to be an estoppel to the consummation of the purchase, was bought off, not by settling it, but by getting those in charge to stop proceedings.[49]

The *Sun* published the *Spy* article on December 9, and other papers quickly reprinted or commented upon it.[50] A number of editors and reporters discounted the allegations and expressed resentment at the implication that journalists were involved in a payoff. Their attempts at rebuttal uncovered additional information about the lobby. "Some wretched Bohemian started the story," which was fed by "the lively imagination of a newspaper scribbler," complained the *New York Herald*'s Washington correspondent. Three days later the same reporter attacked "this ridiculous story of $2,200,000 having been used" and stated that banker Riggs had received only "a very trifling commission" of "some $7,000 or $8,000." He also boldly asserted that the young "Colonel" — a reference to Robert Martin — who claimed to have a list of the parties paid off was "simply a blackmailer."[51]

The *New York World*'s Washington correspondent, himself named by the *Spy* as one of those reportedly paid off, predicted that C.C. Washburn or another congressman would ask for a select committee of investigation. He disclosed further that Robert J. Walker had been employed as counsel by the Russian government and would demand an investigation "in view of recent sensational reports." The *World*'s editors joined the clamor for an official inquiry, "beginning with an examination of Congressman Baldwin," the *Spy*'s proprietor.[52]

Uriah Painter, distressed at the unexpected turn of events, worked actively to discredit the *Spy*'s report and Martin's stories. He still contended that Riggs had gotten a loan of $200,000 in greenbacks; however, he concluded as a result of tracing the several checks to New York banks and examining the cancelled checks that no congressman or journalist had endorsed them. He also confessed that

Treasurer Spinner knew nothing of the use of the money and asserted that the figures bandied about by Martin were wild. Painter even defended Walker, reporting that he admitted receiving a fee "for his professional services" and was annoyed at the envy of those whom the governor said "failed to get a slice."[53]

The *Sun's* editor conceded at last that Walker had been involved but was "the only lobby agent yet known." Forgetting what actually occurred in August, Dana recalled inaccurately that Walker "was robbed in an omnibus in this city of a gold check for $25,000," and noted that one of the Treasury checks received by Riggs was for that amount. He speculated that Walker "may have lost a gold check for $25,000 representing that identical money." A congressional investigation "is now impossible to prevent," the editor asserted, but he voiced confidence "that no member of Congress was bribed at all, just as we are confident that no respectable journal received a cent from this most unpleasant fund." No doubt the lobbyists had walked off with the money while pretending "to bribe their friends in Congress and the press. The folly, the absurdity of this use of the two hundred thousand dollars is glaringly demonstrated by the identification with it of Mr. Robert J. Walker. There is not a man in the country who has less influence than he."[54]

The burst of unhappy comments by reporters and the editorial pleas for an investigation impelled Congress to respond. The *New York Herald* reported "a race" by "a half dozen members" of the House of Representatives on December 14 to introduce a resolution. A prominent Democrat won the honors. Representative Fernando Wood had been notoriously corrupt during his several terms as mayor of New York City, when he was a mentor by example for his enemy and political successor, William M. Tweed. Wood was sensitive, however, to the feelings of the affronted New York newspapers, especially the Democratic *World*. His resolution consisted of a lengthy extract from the *Spy's* article followed by a single sentence referring the matter to the Committee on Public Expenditures for investigation. The clever measure, which was quickly adopted without opposition under a suspension of the rules, encompassed Treasurer Spinner, Riggs, Walker, and various newspapers and journalists. It did not mention congressmen, who were thus neatly omitted from the committee's required scrutiny.[55]

The press was pleased at being afforded the opportunity to respond to charges, and overlooked the omission. Even Wood's peren-

nial critic, the *New York Tribune*, thanked him "for one good deed."
Now, said the paper, "let us see who got the two hundred thousand
dollars for influencing Congressmen, and how the Congressmen will
continue to treat the financial worthies after their blushing honors
have been revealed." The *Herald's* Washington reporter thought
that none of the allegations mentioned by the *Spy* would be substan-
tiated but quoted Ben Butler as believing "there is more in the stories
than is generally supposed" and said that he would keep a sharp
eye on the proceedings.[56]

Typically in American public life, sensational stories breed more
of the kind until the appetite is sated. In the instance of the Alaska
scandal, another misleading rumor surfaced just as New York Republican Calvin T. Hulburd, chairman of the Committee on Public
Expenditures, prepared to open his committee's inquiry. The *New
York Tribune, Sun,* and *Herald,* among other newspapers, published
reports that Caleb Cushing, a well-known expansionist politician
and diplomat, had been rewarded for lobbying on behalf of Alaska
by a special foreign assignment. (Some versions had it that Cushing
originally had expected a legation and been disappointed.) Cushing
had gone abroad, but none of the papers knew where. There were
speculations about Samaná, Tehuantepec, and Bogotá. The *Sun* conjectured that he might have been sent to Madrid to buy Cuba for
$100 million in gold, for which he carried a draft. "If this be true,
we hope that he will not lose the draft in a New York omnibus,
as Robert J. Walker lost his famous fee as an Alaska lobby agent."
The *Tribune* thought that the matter should be investigated.

The facts were simple enough. President Johnson — still afflicted
with dreams of diplomatic triumphs despite the approaching end
of his administration — appointed Cushing as special minister to Co-
lombia upon Senator Sumner's recommendation. The purpose of
his secret mission was to negotiate a treaty for a ship-canal route
across the Isthmus of Panama. Cushing completed his assignment
and returned in late February 1869. The Senate eventually ratified
the treaty, but it was never employed. Cushing's mysterious mission served only to fix public impressions of wrongdoing on Alaska.[57]

One more person was needed to complete the list of characters
for a convincing theory of conspiracy. This was Thurlow Weed. His
name first appeared publicly in connection with Alaska at the time
of Senate ratification of the treaty in April 1867 and was tied to
the lobby occasionally thereafter, even for such preposterous sums

as $250,000. In the spring of 1868 Ben Butler tried to link him to the Whisky Ring, and Weed figured simultaneously in the Alta Vela controversy. It was, however, his long association with the secretary of state that prompted the *New York Herald* on December 15 to ask that "Seward's old State barber," along with the secretary, Walker and the correspondents, be placed under oath, and that Stoeckl also be asked for an explanation.[58] Weed could not have figured significantly in lobbying for the appropriation bill. He was sick during much of May and June and became seriously ill on June 26. He was stricken again on July 3 and revived only enough to sail for Europe the following week in search of a more complete recovery. He did not return until well after the election.[59] But the stories about him deepened suspicions of dishonest dealings involving Alaska.

Russian Minister Edouard de Stoeckl. Reproduced from the Collections of the Library of Congress.

Secretary of State William H. Seward. Reproduced from *Seward at Washington* (1891).

President Andrew Johnson. Reproduced
from the Collections of the Library of
Congress.

Senator Charles Sumner. Reproduced
from the Collections of the Library of
Congress.

Representative Nathaniel P. Banks. Reproduced from the Collections of the Library of Congress.

Representative Thaddeus Stevens. Reproduced from *Republicanism in America* (1869).

Representative Benjamin F. Butler. Reproduced from the Collections of the Library of Congress.

Representative C.C. Washburn. Reproduced from the Collections of the Library of Congress.

Representative Elihu B. Washburne. Reproduced from the Collections of the Library of Congress.

Legal Counsel Robert J. Walker. Reproduced by permission of the Kansas State Historical Society.

Associate Counsel Frederick P. Stanton. Reproduced by permission of the Kansas State Historical Society.

Democratic Campaign Manager Samuel J. Tilden. Reproduced from *Life of Samuel J. Tilden* (1876).

Editor Horace Greeley. Reproduced
from *Recollections of a Busy Life* (1868).

Editor Charles A. Dana. Reproduced
from the Collections of the Library of
Congress.

Editor John W. Forney. Reproduced
from *The Life of Horace Greeley* (1873).

CHAPTER THREE

THE ALASKA INVESTIGATION
AND THE TARNISHING OF AMERICAN EXPANSIONISM

The standing Committee on Public Expenditures, which had other work to complete before the Fortieth Congress ended on March 3, 1869, interpreted its assignment narrowly under the Wood resolution. The members immediately summoned Treasurer Francis Spinner and banker George Riggs, both of whom testified on December 16. Armed with Treasury warrants and receipts, Spinner traced the series of withdrawals and argued convincingly that he had handled the transactions properly. He also said that he knew of no payments for lobbying.[1]

Riggs explained that he had transmitted $7,035,000 to the attorney of Baring Brothers and Company in New York, less his own commission of ¹⁄₂₀ of 1 percent, which came to $3,517. He denied ever receiving any greenbacks or ever discussing them with any Treasury official. He had given $26,000 in gold to Robert J. Walker, whom Stoeckl told him was paid as counsel to the Russian legation. He transferred the remaining $139,000 in several payments to the minister, whose presence in New York City had delayed completion of the transaction until September. He could not explain why Stoeckl did not take all the money in one sum, but he had heard of heavy expenses, including $10,000 in gold for one lengthy telegraph message to Russia.[2]

Most papers carried factual reports of the first testimony, and comments were subdued. Two prominent papers confirmed public suspicions by questioning what the committee could uncover. The *New York Tribune*, noting that the lobbyists would testify next, predicted "that those gentry will prove equal to the occasion" and keep "a monopoly" of anything they know. The *Washington Evening Star* contended that only Stoeckl, who would be exempt from being called even if he were in the country, could account for his expenditures. As a consequence, "the country will be little wiser at the close of the investigation than it is now."[3]

The *New York Herald*, in contrast, bluntly concluded that "a goodly slice" of the appropriation went for the lobby, since this was "the way things are done at the national capital . . . the banker, Mr. Riggs, acknowledges that he had the money. . . . Robert J. Walker acknowledges the corn." Publisher James Gordon Bennett's editors did not spare other papers, moreover, singling out the rival *Tribune* for particular criticism:

> The newspapers are in it. The Tribune of this city is put down as provided for in two separate sums . . . The correspondents of the Times, World and Post of this city are said to have come in for the dribbling of this cash . . . proportionate no doubt to the influence of these sheets. The Washington Chronicle, the Boston Journal, the Boston Advertiser, the Philadelphia Press and the Chicago Tribune are all in the list. Washington correspondents are often bought, and the editors of the papers that are implied in the bargain cannot help it. . . . [There is] no great prejudice to any sheets except the Washington paper and the Tribune of this city [because it was] bought in this city as well as in Washington . . . its very active hostility to the Alaska purchase became a very gentle and gingerly opposition toward the close of the transaction.

The arrival of a Danish minister eager to sell St. Thomas will afford "the lobbymen, correspondents, and others" a new opportunity, the *Herald* confided. A second editorial suggested that Denmark might turn over the management of its treaty to the lobby for half price, for "there are politicians in Washington who are on the qui vive for the main chance."[4]

The committee continued its hearings on Alaska for almost two months following the appearances of Skinner and Riggs.[5] It is instructive to review the key testimony before considering again the reactions of the press. Robert J. Walker was the first prominent witness. The self-assured lawyer, who promised to divulge "even confidential communications" with Minister Stoeckl despite the "very sacred" relationship with his client, recounted that he had written expansionist pamphlets before Stoeckl employed him in May 1868 for similar work. He had refused to "lobby" and had not "called upon" any congressmen except Banks, to seek a copy of his report on the measure, and Sumner, to inquire about the difficulty over the House's powers. He "never paid or offered to pay" a dollar to any member of Congress. After the bill's passage, Stoeckl voluntarily gave him $1,000 in gold and $2,300 in greenbacks in addition

to his promised fee of $20,000 in gold—plus another $5,000 in greenbacks for his associate counsel, Frederick Stanton. (Stoeckl's total
payment to Walker and Stanton came to almost $26,000 in gold,
since $100 in gold was worth about $150 in greenbacks.) Walker
later suggested that Stoeckl pay $3,000 in gold to Colonel John For-
ney, editor of the *Daily Morning Chronicle*, in appreciation for the
space given his articles; Forney declined to take the money, so Walker
gave it to D.C. Forney, the Colonel's brother and publisher of the
paper. He did not know what Stoeckl had done with the remainder
of the Alaska payment—though the envoy had complained of "enormous" telegraph charges—but he was confident that no other
member of the press or of Congress had gotten "one dollar" either
"directly or indirectly."[6] The committee failed to ask its voluble witness about being robbed in New York, so that misleading incident
was not cleared up. Walker divulged under oath, however, that
Stoeckl had employed him as counsel and spent $29,000 gold in fees
and gifts. Beyond these things he said little. The committee never
called the Forneys.

The day's second witness was veteran reporter W.W. Warden,
who also served President Johnson as a secretary and congressional
liaison agent. Warden stated that he had written articles on behalf
of the appropriation. He also had reported the rumors of money
being spent; but he had discovered no foundation for these tales
among the dozen newsmen he queried and was "sorry" that he "had
been omitted" himself if "there was any money to be paid."[7] His
refuge in rumors and defense of the press set the pattern for the
reporters who testified later.

Next came the *Worcester Spy*'s correspondent, R.J. Hinton, who
had written the sensational dispatch of December 7. He explained
that his story merely had been an account of reports afloat and that
he had heard allegations for months. On one occasion, James R.
Young of the *New York Tribune* told him that a Mr. Martin had
approached him that very morning with a list of newspapermen
supposed to have received payments; other correspondents "all in-
timated, more or less, their belief that there was foundation" for
the stories circulating. Reporter W.B. Shaw had told him about
Riggs's connection, Walker was mentioned "frequently," and there
was talk of Forney "having received money." His impression was
that neither Young nor any of the reporters mentioned received

anything but that "some middleman had made believe he had influence with the press, and had thus obtained money."[8]

Before the *Tribune's* Young appeared, the committee heard William H. Seward. The secretary of state did not mention the story he had told President Johnson and John Bigelow several months before. Instead, he said that he knew "nothing whatever of the use the Russian minister made of the fund." Seward had encouraged the work of Walker, with whom he conferred "very freely upon all public questions" and "of whose patriotism, intelligence, and industry" he had "a very high estimate." He was aware that Stoeckl, too, appreciated Walker's efforts. But Seward never heard *from Walker* that "he was to have" $25,000. Asked whether "any" fund had been employed with the press, the secretary answered narrowly that the Department of State had not spent more than $500 for the negotiation and paid nothing "to subsidize any press anywhere."[9]

Seward did inform the committee, which had invited Russian Secretary Waldemar Bodisco to appear, that the diplomat "was not authorized by his Government to enter into any conversation on this subject."[10] Bodisco simultaneously disclosed to reporters "that Mr. Stoeckl alone knows what was done with the money."[11] Later testimony proved Bodisco's statement false, and the committee foundered on the lack of information from the Russian legation.

Frederick P. Stanton, Walker's associate counsel, followed Seward as a witness. He attested frankly that he had conversed with congressmen such as Thad Stevens and General Robert Schenck of Ohio — but not with many other members, because he thought the appropriation "almost certain to pass." His dealings with Stoeckl had been through Walker. He was aware of the payment to Forney but of no others. His own modest retainer of $5,000 in greenbacks would have been "a very contemptible amount" with which "to buy" congressmen. Uriah Painter had confronted him some weeks earlier with the assertion that Riggs paid "about thirty thousand dollars each," presumably to congressmen; but he questioned Painter's refusal to disclose how he got that information.[12] Stanton unsurprisingly volunteered nothing about the offer made on his behalf to Samuel Tilden on July 13, 1868, that the Washington press corps was "in an organized State" and could be purchased for $3,000 to $3,500 a month.[13] Democratic party leader Tilden possessed this damaging letter but did not come forward to testify.

The committee next heard *New York Tribune* reporter James R. Young, the brother of the paper's managing editor, who stated that he and other newsmen had written about the Alaska rumors. After he published a story on a possible congressional investigation, he said, a southerner named Martin approached him and wanted to provide information; the man stated that he had worked for Walker and been cheated of his share. Young had talked at length to Martin, who claimed to have names, affidavits, and copies of checks but would not show them. One such list put Young himself down for $5,000 and his paper for $20,000. He had as a result concluded that Martin was "foolish" or "deceived," an "adventurer or loafer," since he never had received or been promised any money. Horace Greeley likewise had thought it "very singular" for the *Tribune* to be charged with receiving money after its persistent opposition to the purchase.[14]

Queried by the committee about a reporter named Noah, Young said that he was well acquainted with him but "never heard him say that he got any money." As will be seen, the committee knew more about Noah than Young did. This became clear in the course of testimony by W. Scott Smith, the manager of the Evening Press Association. Smith explained to the committee that Robert Noah frequently had told him of getting Alaska money amounting to $2,000, half of which went to his brother, who represented the *New York Democrat* recently established by political boss "Brick" Pomeroy. Noah had referred to "a fund set aside for the press" — some $200,000 — with which Walker was connected. As for himself, Smith declared that he had not received "a cent."[15]

Following the Christmas recess, the committee summoned Uriah Painter of the *New York Sun* and *Philadelphia Inquirer*. He related at length that he had learned of Stoeckl's peculiar withdrawals of the payment by talking with Treasurer Skinner and by checking the official records. He had then spoken freely to congressmen about "an improper influence at work." He also had confronted Stanton about Walker's role and seen him on the floor of Congress. Painter admitted, though, that he lacked "specific information," knew of no member of Congress or the press who had received money, and thought that there were "middle-men" who "sold the press out." He received no money himself because he had opposed the purchase with "unrelenting hostility" — a somewhat exaggerated claim.[16]

Painter testified much as did other reporters. He soon came under attack, however, and was called back as the central figure of suspicion.

The next witness was editor Robert Noah of the *New York Democrat*. He denied W. Scott Smith's allegation that he had received $2,000 from Walker, whom he had never seen. What had happened, he said, was that his brother, M.M. Noah (whom Smith had identified incorrectly), the editor of the *San Francisco Alta California*, furnished much information to the Committee on Foreign Relations about Russian laws, the fisheries, and the fur trade. Robert Noah explained that, after Congress passed the appropriation, Secretary Bodisco greeted his brother on the street with word that Stoeckl had directed that he be given $1,000 in greenbacks for his services. M.M. Noah had not expected such a gift, hoping rather to become governor if Alaska were made a territory. Robert Noah observed that he had not even known that Stanton, his "next-door neighbor," was connected with the affair until he read about it. The committee, which published only part of his testimony, did not ask him about a discrepant version of the brothers' contacts with Bodisco published earlier in the *Rochester Chronicle* and *Washington Evening Star*, and the panel did not summon M.M. Noah or ever recall Smith.[17]

Chairman Hulburd's absence in mid-January further weakened the inquiry, and the committee stumbled over an allegedly missing key witness. Young of the *Tribune*, who had testified about the mysterious James Martin, and other correspondents reported on January 8 and 9 that the committee had issued him a summons. Interest mounted when Martin did not appear.[18]

By January 12, the *New York Herald* reported that the committee was "exceedingly anxious" to see Martin but had been unable to find him. This news surprised Martin, who assured the *Herald*'s man that he had given the committee his address and was eager to talk. The *Herald* also reported a rumor that Martin had gone to Seward to discuss the purchase money and that the secretary of state would say nothing to him without the Russian minister present. "The absent witness is no myth" but is "awaiting to hear from the committee," the *Herald* announced.

Three days later the paper ran another long story, saying that Martin boasted of "very damaging information" if the committee

desired "to pump him." Martin had told the *Herald* that Seward
"pooh-poohed" his stories, then offered him "a secret mission to Mex-
ico." "According to Martin's statement" to the *Herald*, Stoeckl had
offered "a half million of dollars" to Thad Stevens, but "the good
old man refused any recompense." A prominent "Eastern member
[Banks] was found to take charge," while "another Eastern member
[Butler] scented the game. He had a small claim on the Russian
government." Stoeckl's expenditures included: "To an ex-public
printer, [Cornelius Wendell] $5,000; to a near relative of the Great
Commoner, $40,000; to an ex-Commissioner of Pensions, $10,000;
to the Washington correspondent of a New York radical morning
paper, $5,000; to a Washington correspondent . . . known to be at-
tached to a Cincinnati paper, $10,000; to a conservative morning
paper in Baltimore, $20,000; to the Washington special correspon-
dent of the same paper, $5,000; to a Chicago democratic morning
paper, $5,000; to a representative of the Jones family, $10,000; to
an Eastern Senator who had influence with a prominent journal,
$20,000; and the Eastern member . . . No.1, $250,000 . . . No.2,
$150,000. The diplomatic chief [Seward] fell heir to $200,000, and
the great king of the New York lobby [Weed] the modest little sum
of $500,000." The *Herald* conceded that it was "an extravagant story
throughout" but unhesitatingly published the slanderous account.
Meanwhile, the *Washington National Republican* reported suspiciously on January 22 that the committee's sergeant-at-arms, bearing a subpoena, could not find Martin, although he was in Washington all the time![19]

Martin finally appeared on January 23, just as the committee was
beginning a hurried investigation of Wells, Fargo mail contract
frauds. There is no official record of his testimony, but several papers
reported that Martin declared that all he knew came from a former
clerk in the Department of State named Louis Fitzgerald Tasistro.[20]

Tasistro was called at once and came unwillingly. A cultured man,
at home in several languages, he once edited a New York literary
weekly and later wrote books on the southern states and the position of women. In 1866 he published two little volumes on protocol
and etiquette in Washington. Seward employed him at this time
as a clerk in the Department of State, then discharged him but obtained another position for him in the Department of Interior. His
supervisor in Interior, Judge N.S. Howe, wrote Nathaniel Banks
that Tasistro "never forgave Mr. Seward the discharge." He was,

however, "a man of poetry & imagination, a genial & intelligent companion — but of little practical sense." Tasistro's interest in the Perkins claim drew him into the Alaska affair. He had come into possession of the original text of the claim, translated other documents, and been associated with Perkins counsel Joseph B. Stewart. His removal from the State Department lessened his ability to advance the claim and to collect the large fee that he had been promised.[21] Frustrated but imaginative, he circulated stories about the purchase money and stirred the curiosity of Martin and several correspondents.

The committee never released Tasistro's testimony, but many correspondents covered his appearance. Tasistro told the panel that he considered the purchase "a great swindle" because Alaska could have been bought years before for $5 million. After the purchase, when he sardonically congratulated the Russian minister, Stoeckl had responded, "My dear Tasistro, only five millions of the money come to us." The witness believed that Seward, Banks, and Butler had gotten the balance. He maintained that the secretary of state paid off a large mortgage on his property in Auburn, New York; that General Banks, who had left the army poor, invested heavily in real estate; and that General Butler, who was pledged to settle the Perkins claim, ceased work after money was paid to his friends.[22]

The weary committee gave little consideration to Tasistro's account or motives, since the members were anxious to turn to the Wells, Fargo probe and unaware of the extent of his connection with the Perkins claim. Judge Howe, who was "amazed at Tasistro's Alaska testimony," privately assured Banks that his former clerk "would quite as readily & confidently believe you had rcvd of this fruit, from the fact that you had paid some old debts, as if he had heard the bargain & seen the coin in your hands. His testimony will excite but laughter in those who know him, & I venture to say he 'smiled' immediately after leaving the witness stand, if not before."[23]

The laughter, however, was muffled. James Martin, who was recalled immediately, confirmed that Tasistro had told him the same story. Martin added that he first learned of the affair from a news item and from a Coloradan named T.M. Ford, who asserted that congressmen had received large payments and Banks some $250,000. Tasistro had displayed a copy of a letter he wrote to Secretary Bodisco and told Martin of seeing a letter in the State Department from Banks complaining that someone in the Russian legation was "telling tales out of school." Martin stated that Cornelius Wendell was another mentioned as having received money. Wendell had ridiculed this story when Martin asked him, then said that Martin knew too much and would talk no more about it. Martin's mention of Wendell should have sparked further inquiry. A notorious influence peddler who enjoyed lucrative government printing contracts during the Buchanan administration, Wendell almost brought down that President when he garrulously admitted to the Covode investigating committee in 1860 that he had paid out more than $100,000 to Democratic organizers, editors, and congressmen to buy elections and secure the passage of legislation.[24] But the Alaska panel did not summon this patron of so many congressmen.

Robert J. Walker was aroused, however, and asked to respond to charges against "persons high in office made on very wretched authority." After he appeared earlier, he informed the committee, "those accusations have got into the newspapers and before the public, and some of the gentlemen against whom they have been preferred insist that I shall testify as to certain things." Walker ignored the fact that similar reports had appeared widely *before* his first testimony, and he did not explain why he must speak for the others.

The feisty witness maligned Martin's credibility. His account was that Martin had stopped him on the street prior to the meeting of Congress in December. Walker had agreed to speak briefly to him in Willard's Hotel, where Martin told him that Seward, Banks, and Butler received large sums and that Democratic Representative Samuel Randall of Pennsylvania had obtained a share. Walker had retorted that such statements were "perfectly absurd," that Butler had "come near defeating" the measure, and that this was all "a continuation of the black-mailing operations" begun before the bill was passed. When Martin referred to an incriminating letter from Banks to the secretary of state, Walker had called it "a most infamous falsehood;" Martin, after fumbling in his papers, declined to produce the document. Walker suggested that the committee examine Stanton, Seward, and General George P. Este, to whom Martin had made similar statements. He then challenged the statement of W. Scott Smith of the Evening Press Association that he had paid $2,000 to the Noah brothers. Noah himself had since testified that he received $1,000 "but not from me." He had known nothing about this before reading the testimony.

Walker next struck at Uriah Painter. When the appropriation was pending, he recalled, Frederick Stanton had come to him with word that Painter offered, for some of the Russian money, to influence the press and control votes; Walker had responded that he "had no money for any such purpose." A few days later Stanton reported that Painter angrily threatened to defeat the bill. Walker had become "excited," said again there was no such money, would quit the case "if any money were used in that way to carry the bill," and would kick Painter out of his office if he ever appeared with such a proposition. After this investigation began, Walker concluded, Robert Latham informed Stanton and himself that Painter threatened to destroy Stanton if those offers were disclosed. Stanton had "pooh-poohed the idea."[25]

The panel then recalled Stanton, turning the entire focus of its inquiry upon the role of Painter. Stanton elaborated the account of Painter's offer to influence votes and later threats of retaliation. Walker's associate counsel also related that Painter had confronted him once more after Walker was robbed, when the reporter had claimed that Walker was "going to the Fifth Avenue Hotel" to distribute the money, presumably to congressmen. Stanton had revealed to Painter that Walker received around $20,000 but gave none of it to members of Congress; Painter had said that he knew better and that $2 million had been used. On still another occasion Painter had told a disbelieving Stanton that Riggs & Company put out the money in sums of $30,000, to the wife of a congressman and to others — that "the damned rascals" in the deal had lied to him and he would "now expose them" because they refused to employ him. Stanton had warned Painter that he would only expose himself — as the witness could now demonstrate to the committee. Stanton fended off queries as to why he had carried messages to Walker from Painter and perhaps led the reporter on. He confided that he had always been on friendly terms with Painter but that reporters, "if they were disposed to make mischief, could make a good deal of it." From the beginning, he insisted, Walker "indignantly rejected the idea of employing and paying" Painter.[26]

Acting Chairman John Broomall concluded that much of the Washington press corps was not trustworthy. On the day after Stanton's second appearance, W. Scott Smith testified as the committee resumed its inquiry into the Wells, Fargo mail-contract frauds. The manager of the Evening Press Association urged the committee to look further into rumors he had heard. Broomall, a Delaware Republican who had not sought reelection in 1868 and would retire from Congress within a month, exploded angrily that there were "certain correspondents" who "probably deserve to be stigmatized as engaging in jobs" because they manufactured stories "for the purpose of blackmail." He "would not believe any correspondent in Washington under oath." Any reporter "who remained in Washington for even two weeks got thoroughly corrupted." When first-term Pennsylvania Democrat J. Lawrence Getz defended the newsmen, saying that he considered a reporter's oath "as good as that of a member of Congress or any other man," Broomall snapped that praise from a correspondent would give the public grounds for suspecting a member's honesty. Insinuations and denials by other reporters followed Broomall's flare-up, until the Wells, Fargo investigation nearly collapsed two days later, on February 6.[27]

All the while there was a flurry of activity in the Alaska affair. Some congressmen and reporters had anticipated that Stanton's testimony on February 3 would end the inquiry. Uriah Painter, however, voluntarily returned to the committee on the following day and repudiated Stanton's testimony entirely.[28] On February 5 he wrote to the *New York Tribune* to complain angrily about its publication of a dispatch that was "a wicked libel" on him since he had denied Stanton's statements under oath. "If a man's character is to be so assailed on no evidence at all," he protested, "who is safe a day from the malice of men who by their own admissions are corrupt?"[29] His reference was to Stanton's admission of service as associate counsel to Stoeckl.

Stanton at once countered Painter's denial by writing a letter on February 6 to Chairman Hulburd. He urged that Robert W. Latham, who was to testify that day, be asked to clear up key points: Painter's use of Latham to seek employment and pay from Walker; Painter's threat to attack Stanton if their conversations were revealed; and the existence of an affidavit seen or possessed by Painter alleging that Walker had withheld $25,000 to $30,000 which was to have been paid to Painter and other press agents. "Latham knows to what extent Mr. Painter has admitted the truth of my statements," Stanton said in his letter, which he released to reporters.[30]

Publisher W.W. Harding of the *Philadelphia Inquirer* watched the growing controversy closely. After Stanton's testimony he wired Painter: "How would it do to have S. arrested at once for perjury? If he commences private lying under oath he had better learn a public lesson. Answer." When Stanton's letter appeared in the *Philadelphia Bulletin* and other papers, Harding wired anxiously on the evening of February 7: "What do you think of it?" The reporter apparently responded that Harding should publish an article prepared for the *New York Sun* and complained of opposition from Colonel Forney. Just before midnight, Harding sent a second telegram: "What evidence have you of Forney being against you? Is not Latham willing to give you an affidavit? This will completely demolish Fred Stanton's statement as he now throws the "onus" on Latham's statement of what you would do."[31]

Latham had already appeared earlier that day. He testified almost exclusively about Painter, and the committee shared his interest. Stanton's confrere told how the correspondent had tried several times to learn from him if Walker, Stanton, and Latham himself were involved in the Alaskan affair for fees and if there had been payments to reporters. Latham repeatedly disavowed the slightest personal interest. He took no notice, he said, of Painter's warnings of an investigation and found Stanton's explanation for not revealing his role prior to the investigation "entirely satisfactory." In the company of Stanton he had told Walker of Painter's allegations and enjoyed the governor's "exceedingly eloquent" denunciation of Martin and reporters, but it was not his way ever to "mix with these matters." (His diffident manner contrasted sharply with his insistent letter to Samuel Tilden on July 13, 1868, when he urged the Democratic leader to provide Stanton with thousands of dollars to purchase the Washington press corps.) The shrewd Latham avoided seriously implicating Painter, who was already in enough difficulty. The reporter "did not say that he wished to be employed," Latham conceded, but only meant to see "what was being done." Painter had not even said that he would write articles about what he learned, though he had promised to attack Stanton if their conversation became known. When the inquisitive Broomall asked if Painter was "industrious," Latham agreed that the correspondent, whom he had known for ten years, was "about the most industrious reporter there is in town" and was ready to "do almost anything" to get the information he wanted.[32]

Painter, who was listening, let the committee know that he was ready to answer any questions and denied again ever having asked for a share of the money.[33] On Monday, February 8, he came before the panel for the third time. His appearance marked an ironic end to his own work. The brash reporter who had done more than anyone to expose wrongdoing in the Alaskan affair had to clear himself. "Your correspondent will be completely vindicated," he wrote that morning, "and the country left in the dark as to where all the money went."[34]

As the session developed, the committee showed no interest in tracing Alaskan payments, and Broomall grilled him: What had transpired with Stanton? Why had he sought information? Why was he so earnest to know? What other efforts had he made? Why did he want to learn whether there was money in it? Did he seek to be employed? What evidence of fraud did he have? Had he misled Stanton about his intentions? Did he know Martin and keep in touch with him?[35]

Painter was on the defensive throughout, though not apologetic. He related once more his suspicions of Walker, his belief that the purchase was "a big swindle" and "one of Seward's jobs," and his determination to tear it all "to pieces." To take part himself would have destroyed his "honor and reputation." When he mentioned again the Walker robbery as proof of fraud, Broomall interjected sharply that his question "had reference to facts and not to newspaper articles." Painter admitted that he knew nothing more than he had stated in previous hearings. But he could not have misled Stanton, he insisted, and he never heard of Martin before the affair and "very soon lost credence in his statements" as he wrote in his articles. Broomall's suggestion that he might have been in league with Martin must have been particularly galling, for Painter vigorously denied "any intercourse with him, either by letter or in any other shape or form."[36]

Then Representative Getz was at him, asking once more whether he had said to Stanton in any way that he wanted a share if there was any money for the press. Ignoring Painter's rejoinder that he had said only that Walker kept the money himself if there were any for newspapermen, Democrat Getz tried repeatedly to belittle the entire affair as a misunderstood joke. Hadn't the reporters said in jest that they would like to share in any money circulating? Might Painter himself have talked in that way? Had he spoken in jest to Stanton?[37]

Painter denied his inquisitor's implications. He defended his colleagues and the seriousness of the investigation he had begun. There was jesting among the correspondents, he admitted, but men should not be held responsible for that. He had not spoken in jest and "certainly not" to Stanton.[38] With this exchange the public hearings came to an inconclusive end, as congressional investigations often do.

The press usually reports only the spectacular moments in congressional inquiries; the public pays even less attention to such goings on and quickly puts them out of mind when they are at an end. The Alaska inquiry, however, drew more than the usual notice — and left a greater residue of suspicion. The chief reason why the Alaska affair created extraordinary reverberations was that it touched the integrity of many major newspapers and leading Washington reporters. The press maintained considerable interest in the hearings despite their protracted length and other exciting news, including major new frauds in New York, President Johnson's controversial pardons of prominent Confederates, and preparations for Ulysses S. Grant's inauguration.

Four popular New York papers — the *Sun, World, Tribune,* and *Herald* — ran well over sixty articles and editorials on the inquiry between mid-December and early February. The *Times* (a supporter of Seward), the *Commercial Advertiser* (Thurlow Weed's paper), the *Evening Post,* and other newspapers added greatly to the number of stories that appeared in New York. Four Washington dailies — the *Morning Chronicle, National Intelligencer, National Republican,* and *Evening Star* — carried at least thirty articles and editorials in the same period. The coverage would have been greater had not the *Chronicle* halted its reports on the investigation after Robert J. Walker testified that publisher D.C. Forney had received a payment of $3,000 in gold. (The paper never mentioned that revelation, and the editor, Colonel Forney, shortly left Washington for a tour of southern states.) There was extensive coverage in Baltimore and Philadelphia papers, with some stories even in Forney's *Philadelphia Press.* Interested dailies from the *Worcester Spy* to the *San Francisco Alta California* insured that the news carried from coast to coast.[39]

The accounts and editorials varied in length from brief references to reports filling several columns. Only the most casual reader of daily newspapers in late 1868 and early 1869 could have been unaware of allegations that the United States had been defrauded doubly by the corruptly obtained purchase of a worthless region of ice. Similar accounts reached other readers through weekly and semi-weekly papers, some of which were subsidiaries of the daily presses.[40]

Americans often have been told of corruption in their government and commonly believe it. The context of the outgoing Johnson administration gave special meaning to the flood of stories about Alaskan scandals. Tempers remained high in Washington after the failure of impeachment and the election of General Grant. Radical Republicans writhed under the lame-duck presidency, and many other citizens shared the Radicals' publicly expressed views that the administration was dishonest as well as traitorously pro-southern. Fraud and "ring" (meaning a dishonest combination) were current watchwords.

The Internal Revenue Service, which had charge of the heavy whisky taxes and licenses on distillers, was a particular object of suspicion in late 1868, as it had been throughout the year. Scarcely a week passed during the Alaska investigation without reports in major newspapers about suspected whisky frauds or congressional revelations of rings of revenue agents and distillers bilking the government. On December 21, for instance, the *Washington National Republican* published a story about the Alaska testimony of Secretary Seward and John Russell Young, followed by a report on whisky frauds. This was an account of the work of the House Committee on Retrenchment, chaired by General Charles Van Wyck, a New York Republican. The front-page story remarked on the "mass of testimony which will, even in these days of corruption, astound the country." (Still other articles dealt with dishonesty in New York elections and cheating on duties for imported silk.) The *New York Tribune* editorialized cynically that day about the findings of the Van Wyck committee, which "tells us that there are frauds in whisky, which everybody knows; that Andrew Johnson is vastly to blame, which everybody believes; and that there are many bad men in the revenue service, which nobody denies." The *New York Herald* simultaneously ran a series of editorials on corruption and identified a number of thieving conspiracies, among them tariff rings, a steamship-subsidy ring, the treasury ring, the whisky ring, the telegraph-monopoly ring, the land-grab ring, and an Indian agents' ring.[41]

Late 1868 and early 1869 was a time of little faith in government. The suspicion of corruption — congressional as well as executive — was genuinely felt, and not merely the work of opportunistic journalists or of frustrated Radical Republicans. A fortnight after James R. Young of the *New York Tribune* appeared as a witness in the Alaska hearings, his brother, Managing Editor John Russell Young, wrote to Representative E.B. Washburne, a bitter opponent of Alaska, Grant's closest confidante in Congress, and a leading prospect for a cabinet position. What was needed from Grant, Young advised, was "Some Hercules in the Interior Department, for instance, who will take the many-headed serpent of robbery and strangle it in its various shapes — Indian Rings, Patent Rings, Stationery Rings, and Railroad Rings. This work will, of course, make a tremendous howl among Congress people." Three days later Washburne received praise from prominent New York businessman Henry Hilton for a speech auguring change. "The people as well as the politicians," Hilton wrote, "should know that on March 4th commences the reign of honesty and economy . . . that Stealing must then cease and whiskey rings must then be dissolved."[42]

All the while, major newspapers of varied political persuasions maintained the onslaught against governmental corruption. A few examples for January and February 1869 will suffice. The independent *New York Herald* called for an end to the "sucking power" of such "leeches" as the Western Union Telegraph monopoly ring, the railroad subsidy ring, the Canadian reciprocity ring, and the Freedmen's Bureau ring. The Republican *New York Tribune* warned that "the whiskey ring is strong in the Senate. It will not repeal the Tenure of Office Act because that would give General Grant an opportunity to oust the whiskey revenue thieves and to purify the government." The Republican *Washington Evening Star*'s observation that the whisky ring had "applied brains to the business of stealing and swindling" drew concurrence from Forney's *Morning Chronicle* that there was "very great talent and a degree of zeal and industry." Criminals who thrived "under the Johnson Administration," however, would encounter something more than rhetoric when Grant took office.[43]

The editors often knowingly alluded to the Alaskan scandals in their exposes. "The latest ring is the ring of the Mexican dollar," commented the Democratic *New York World*. "Considering the low state of the finances and what hard work Russia had to shame the

Alaska money out of us . . . it would be well to intermit this business
till we have our accounts all straight and can pay for our fancy
stock cash down." Even Forney's pro-Alaska *Philadelphia Press*
grumbled, after hearing of trouble caused by dishonest Indian
agents, "Hardly a year has elapsed since our purchase of Alaska,
and already we have an incipient Indian war on hand. This kind
of thing is getting beyond endurance."[44]

Reporters and editors responded with special vigor to the Alaska
investigation, in large measure because the press itself was on trial.
Allegations of wrongdoing appeared in many articles and editorials,
which often were more incriminating than the actual hearings. The
journalists of that day, as in later times, raised rather than allayed
suspicions. Those newspapermen who were themselves accused
either ignored the charges or proclaimed their innocence; commonly
they sought to place blame elsewhere. The result was to sharpen
the impression of widespread dishonesty.

Forney's papers provide illustrations. Before the *Washington
Morning Chronicle* stopped covering the hearings, it held that the
payments were "legitimate and proper, and that the cries of 'corruption,' 'bribery,' etc., have emanated from those who were
desirious [*sic*] of, but failed to secure, pickings themselves." The
Philadelphia Press adopted the alternative explanation that "some
unauthorized person," pretending to represent the press, obtained
a large sum of money. As the investigation continued, the *Press*
turned against the rival *Inquirer*'s Painter, first calling his testimony
"unimportant," next labelling his behavior "fragrant," and then
falsely reporting that he "acknowledges the main facts given by
Messrs. Walker and Stanton."[45]

Another newspaper that had championed the purchase simply
held the Russians responsible. "If any body paid $2,200,000, or any
other sum, for the passage of the measure through Congress," the
San Francisco Alta California reasoned, "it must have been done
with the knowledge & consent of the Russian Govt." This approach
conceded too much to suit other friends of Alaska and the correspondents who had been inculpated. The *New York World*'s man
took the position that "a scalawag carpetbagger named Martin, from
Alabama" had been "instrumental in circulating the bogus stories."
"It is thought he cannot substantiate any of his allegations," wrote
the *Herald*'s reporter, while Young of the *Tribune* confirmed that
"Martin started the whole scandal." When Painter came under at-

tack, however, Young insisted that his fellow newsman had simply meant to see "if corrupt means were being used."[46]

Even moderate newspapers not accused of involvement in the scandal practiced the journalism of allegation. The *Washington National Republican* admitted that the charges of corruption "excite great interest" among newsmen but argued that "not one of them received a penny." Rather, the paper insinuated, "a 'bummer' named Simon Stephenson, Simon Stapleton (or some such name) whilom a hanger-on around the NY Tribune bureau" had misled Russian Secretary Bodisco and obtained money "to be divided out among the impecunious horde." (The reference to Simon Stevens, well-known lawyer-lobbyist for the Perkins claim, could hardly have been missed.) Two days later the *National Republican* pressed its allegations further, reporting a rumor "in diplomatic circles that a good sum of the Alaska purchase money went to New England, and was there paid out on arms-contracts, with 'margins' for the benefit of parties concerned. It is also generally asserted that F.P. Stanton received a fee for professional advice, and that some of the Pacific coast correspondents were retained." Much the same story — a blend of innuendo, acknowledged facts, and leaks from the committee — appeared in the *New York Herald*.[47]

Another moderate Washington paper, the *Evening Star*, initially took the comfortable view that the payment to Forney was "probably the extent of the connection with the matter" and that there was no evidence of congressional corruption. The *New York Herald* warned, however, against any disposition by the committee "to rest the inquiry," for this would prevent the clearing up of the "sweeping charge" against "other journalists than the Forney firm." When the Noahs' involvement became known a few days later, the *Evening Star* was forced to concede that the committee had not yet gotten "the whole truth."[48]

The scandal continued to weigh on the minds of newspapermen, though some made light of the situation. Ben: Perley Poore, the *Boston Journal's* well-known reporter, who addressed the third annual dinner of the Washington Correspondents Club, complimented his colleagues on their "prosperity during the past year," even if they had "not as yet seen the Russian roubles with which some of their 'enterprising' colleagues of the press has enriched them." But tempers grew thin as the inquiry neared an end. The *New York Sun* sharply attacked the *Tribune* for printing Stanton's statements after Painter

had denied them, while Painter wrote of himself as "the correspondent against whom this conspiracy has been directed."[49]

Painter unhesitatingly broadcast his own suspicions well after the
Alaska hearings commenced. In three successive early reports he
had written that "men of no more influence than Walker bagged
it all;" that the committee was developing information that "large
amounts of money were used by Bodisco in person" beyond what
Walker and others received; and that the reports about the Noahs
were "a blind to get the Committee off the proper trail." Few other
reporters were so aggressive as Painter, but several editors equalled
his insinuations. "Is it not odd," asked the *New York Herald*, "that
Congress waited for a case with Russia to investigate the honesty
of its members on money charges?"[50]

The editors of the Democratic *New York World* likewise were
sarcastic, especially when flaying Republican journalists: "The in-
corruptible Forney indignantly informed the monster that he,
Forney, was like the wife of Caesar . . . and that, on the whole,
the monster had better give the money to Forney's brother. Thus
did the pure Forney preserve his three thousand dollars in gold and
eke his virtue." The *World* sneered, too, at Republican Seward and
"the snowbanks of Alaska," and it argued that "distant detached
possessions are felt to be an expensive encumbrance."[51]

Not even the *World* matched the scorn of the *New York Tribune*
for everything connected with Alaska. Greeley's attacks continued
throughout the investigation: "They have a new name for it in Washington. It is not 'lobbying' but 'acting as counsel'. . . . The Editor
blandly doesn't know, you know, but the Publisher does, and the
cash is paid. . . . What are the duties of a 'counsel' in lobby
cases? . . . One of the latest phrases of modern euphemism is written as 'Lawyers' Fees.' . . . What are we to think of those innu-
merable correspondents who sent the brilliant and glowing account
of Alaska," now called "pleadings" devised by "the teeming brain
of Robert J. Walker, [while] the Czar of all the Russians paid for
them as 'Lawyers' Fees'?" Now that "Baron Stoeckl paid his lawyer's
fees and sent American gold to his master," the United States must
spend more money to set up a civil governor "for the uncivil bears
and walruses." Walker revealed in his return appearance before
the committee that he was "having a good thing [and] didn't want
any partners." As the investigation ended, the *Tribune* sighed,
"Every day brings forth a fresh want of our dear Alaska. This time

it is a District Court to prevent swindling. Oh! If that District Court could only have been established at the outset of the iceberg negotiation."[52]

There were editors, of course, who belittled the inquiry. "The Alaska purchase fraud seems to have dwindled down to a squabble between Mr. F.P. Stanton, claim agent, and Mr. U.H. Painter, newspaper correspondent," the *Washington Evening Star* commented. "This is not what the public bargained for when it was promised developments implicating the Government, Congressmen, and all newspaperdom in being bought over by immense bags of Russian gold." The *Evening Star*, however, waited with interest for the committee's report. Meanwhile, the pro-Seward *New York Times*, which earlier had sniped at the investigation, proclaimed "The Alaska 'Fraud' Fizzle." Even the *Times* concluded suspiciously: "the unfortunate truth is that while, on a false scent, there is always road enough for a full pack to chase, the tortuous, underground work of venality and fraud generally goes on noiselessly, and the tracks are covered up behind."[53] Uriah Painter and Horace Greeley rarely had said it better.

The pack of anti-Alaska journalists did not rest when the Committee on Public Expenditures went into executive session to prepare its report. On February 10, the *New York Tribune*'s correspondents revealed problems in protecting the fur seals, preparations for court trials of violators, and possible starvation among the natives. Greeley's editorial condemned the mounting costs of running the territory.[54]

On the following day, the *New York Sun* announced a possible use for Alaska, though not one to please expansionists. The editor explained that "the alarming increase of crime in New York" and other cities suggested the need for "the institution of a penal colony far away in the Pacific seas" as "a perpetual terror to the criminal population. . . . Providentially we have just bought Alaska! and although as a matter of trade 'tis a bad bargain, and we were egregiously swindled, yet there it lies, far away from us, in the very latitude and longitude most desirable for a penal settlement." It was to be hoped that the people would demand "that the Government shall convert our national icebergs into an American Siberia."[55] Nothing more suitable could be done with Seward's corrupt bargain.

By mid-February the press predicted impatiently that the com-

mittee's report soon would be completed. Days passed and nothing
was forthcoming. News stories appeared disclosing that the committee continued to meet and that a division had developed. The
difficulty was over a proposal to condemn the employment of
lawyers and former members for the purpose of influencing Congress, especially when such lobbyists act "as secret agents of a foreign Govt. against their own."[56]

At last, on February 27, the committee report was ordered to
be printed. There had been a disagreement among the members,
and key differences remained. Chairman Hulburd, two fellow Republicans, and Painter's Democratic inquisitor Getz signed the
document. They reviewed, without questions or criticisms, the statements of Spinner, Riggs, Seward, Walker, Stanton, and Noah about
the use of money in the treaty negotiations. The four members also
reviewed briefly the testimony of R. J. Hinton, whose article in the
Worcester Spy was mentioned in the House resolution establishing
the inquiry. Here the congressmen found fault, commenting on "the
loose morality" of a journalism which "for sensational purposes, or
to cater to a morbid curiosity," linked men with the "clandestine
receipt of large sums of money in connection with votes or influ-
ences." Hinton had "entirely failed to fortify or even at all to justify"
the *Spy*'s article. Other newspapermen, and Martin as well,
disclaimed all personal knowledge and left the committee only with
"nebulous gossip." Neither a reflection nor a suspicion rested on "any
of the presses or persons whose names have been bandied about."[57]
To this point the report whitewashed the leading suspects and much
of the press corps.

Then the committee spent more than a quarter of its report re-
viewing Stanton and Walker's charges against Painter, although the
reporter's "attitude, views or suggestions" were not "necessarily em-
braced within" the House resolution. Painter had testified that he
had always denounced the purchase as a swindle, "and nothing appeared to the contrary," so the committee "did not feel called upon
to further pursue this rather personal and incidental matter" and
now expressed no opinion about it.[58]

In conclusion the members explained that they early had sought
information from the Russian legation in order to "clear away the
clouds of suspicion" or "unerringly indicate" those who trafficked
in the votes of public men or the formation "of public opinion touching that transaction." But relations "with a friendly foreign gov-

ernment" were involved, and the committee lacked "previous proof establishing complicity with criminal acts or purposes." As a result, Russian diplomats could not be asked or cited to appear. The consequence was that the investigation was "*ex parte* in an undesired sense, and consequently barren of affirmative or satisfactory negative results."[59] The admission was a fitting conclusion to a desultory inquiry and tendentious report.

Three other Republican members of the committee, led by the indignant Broomall, and one Democrat prepared a separate, harsher statement directed at Walker and Stanton. The four dissenters expressed "decided disapproval" of "those who permitted themselves to be retained by the Russian minister as advocates or as attorneys for his government in a case in which their own was so deeply interested." Whether it was "right or wrong" for an attorney "to be retained by a foreign power in such a case," the members "deny the morality of his acting upon such retainer without making the fact publicly known" to those with whom he was dealing. "Certainly no man whose former high public position has given him extraordinary influence in the community has the right to sell that influence, the trust and confidence of his fellow-citizens, to a foreign government." No exception was taken to the report's implication that Painter "would have been guilty of a great impropriety" if he had sought secret employment with Stanton and Walker "in the interests of Russia." The failure of the report was in not condemning "those who actually were so employed, and who are at least open to the imputation of endeavoring to divert public attention from their own anomalous position" by directing it towards Painter, "whom they charge with only seeking to be so employed."[60]

The deadlocked committee vote and contradictory reports allayed few suspicions. American politics are often like that. The advantage in March 1869 was that other business could proceed. Congress busied itself with adjournment, and much of the press momentarily turned elsewhere. Correspondents, even for some Radical Republican papers, wrote about the last days of the Johnson administration, though Forney's *Morning Chronicle* ungraciously refused to carry the President's farewell address.[61] There was enormous coverage of Grant's approaching administration.

Uriah Painter and the *New York Sun*, doubtless weary of their Alaskan entanglement, contented themselves with a brief note about the committee report. Forney's Washington and Philadelphia papers provided similar minimal information. The *Worcester Spy*, stung by the committee's criticisms, argued weakly that the testimony proved that Walker had been an agent for Lincoln when he "originated the Alaska sale" and currently received pay from Russia. "Lobby agents rarely succeed in getting paid from both sides."[62]

More substantial articles abounded, despite the competing news in Washington. The *Washington Evening Star*, which then favored short stories, devoted two front-page columns to the Alaska report under the headline, "The Great Question, 'Who Was In It?'" Drawing heavily from the testimony, this paper treated the Painter-Stanton controversy mockingly and found little evidence "of any money having been used to corruptly procure the passage of the measure."[63]

The *New York Herald*, as usual, was more incriminating. James Gordon Bennett's paper, the most sensational of its time, printed the entire Hulburd report on February 27 and the dissenting committee statement the next day, with an editorial to accompany each account. The first *Herald* editorial concluded "that some of the Bohemians in Washington did make desperate efforts" to share in the purchase money. Only Walker was proved to have been paid a fee, but "the balance of two million one hundred and sixty-five thousand dollars appears to have been swallowed up in commissions, fees and costs." Because the committee could not obtain all the information desired, "there still remains a cloud over the Alaska purchase transactions." The second editorial charged that the committee did not have "brains sufficient to fathom the subject" and urged that Baron Stoeckl "publish a card stating how much it cost the Russian government to 'shove through' the Alaska job." If it cost nothing, he should not object to stating the fact and quieting the public. "By his keeping silent we can be assured that where there has been so much smoke there must have been some fire."[64] All indications are that this *Herald* editorial expressed a widely-held view.

Even those citizens who had favored the acquisition of Alaska could now deny any credit to the unpopular Johnson administration. The purchase of Alaska had become a tainted act, and the suspicions were as important as the reality of scandal. The political repercussions were extensive, as was the impact on the popular mind. Expansion in the 1840s had led to sectional strife and the Civil War; expansion in the 1860s involved disreputable dealings.

The current popular interpretation of the purchase — the view that Americans of 1867–1868 saw it as Seward's Folly — doubly misses the historical truth. Not only did many Americans know of Alaska's value (though they later developed more doubts), they thought that the sale was steeped in corruption.

Ulysses S. Grant was inaugurated on Thursday, March 4, 1869. Republicans and many other citizens sighed with relief that the government again was in loyal, honest hands. The Alaska investigation soon passed from the pages of the press. Historians accordingly have seen the purchase as the last gasp of a lame duck administration, and the scandal as a curious but unimportant event. But the scandal was not forgotten just because the Grant administration took office. The involvement of the press and the extended congressional investigation aroused suspicions in Washington, and around the country, of the ulterior motives of expansionists. Memories of the Alaska affair consequently helped to impede one of the new President's interests, acquisition of the Dominican Republic.

CHAPTER FOUR

THE AFTERMATH
OF THE ALASKA SCANDAL

The Civil War did not, as is commonly believed, still the spirit of Manifest Destiny.[1] American expansionists such as Seward, Walker, and Banks were very active again soon after Appomattox. Their interest in Russian America demonstrated the vitality of the desire for more territory. This enthusiasm enabled the otherwise unpopular Johnson administration to win Congress's assent, albeit reluctant, for acquiring this distant and somewhat forbidding land. But the Alaska scandal halted the expansionists' momentum. Widespread reports of lobbying and bribery, and the resulting congressional investigation, established popular suspicions about a dishonest "job."

The extent of the wound inflicted upon American expansionism by the Alaska affair has not been fully appreciated, for several reasons. Although scholars have been aware of the general features of the Alaska scandal, they have treated it as an isolated and, in a few books, rather amusing instance of corruption.[2] They have not investigated the continuing impact of aroused public suspicions or the relation of Alaska to other events, such as Dominican annexation.

With occasional exceptions, historians generally have neglected the issue of corruption in American foreign relations, apparently viewing it as unworthy of notice or unimportant.[3] The pervasive emphasis by both traditional and revisionist historians on diplomacy and policy is understandable, but these factors, important as they are, by no means comprise the whole story. Indeed, during the Gilded Age, prejudices and suspicions often swept aside diplomacy and policy. The same has been true of later eras. The revelations before a Senate committee headed by Senator Gerald Nye during the mid-1930s about alleged warmongering by international bankers and munitions makers dominated political attitudes almost to the eve of the Second World War.[4] In the last few years, events have highlighted again the significance of public suspicions for foreign relations. Vietnam, Watergate, and foreign involvement generally have merged in the popular mind and in political discourse. Middle Eastern policy has become entangled, though to a lesser extent, with arrests of congressmen charged with taking bribes from federal agents disguised as Arab sheikhs and with allegations of payments to the brother of President Jimmy Carter by the Libyan government.[5]

A third reason why the impact of the Alaska affair has been overlooked is that it paled in comparison with the spectacular, prolonged struggle over the proposal to annex the Dominican Republic. The effort initiated by Secretary Seward and pursued vigorously by President Grant to acquire the eastern portion of the island of Santo Domingo set off the most dramatic political controversy over American foreign relations between the Civil War and the crisis with Spain after 1895. Grant's determined campaign for Dominican annexation has, in fact, only one parallel in the entire history of American foreign relations, the effort of President Woodrow Wilson to secure ratification of the Treaty of Versailles with United States membership in the League of Nations. Grant was defeated, as was Wilson after him, despite prodigious efforts and stirring battles in the Senate. His failure, like Wilson's fifty years later, affected the course of American politics and foreign policy for the subsequent two decades. In the instance of the defeat of Dominican annexation, expansionism received a setback from which it never fully recovered, except perhaps briefly at the end of the century.

That the wrenching Dominican affray has overshadowed the Alaskan episode nevertheless is ironical because the purchase of Alaska involved vastly more territory and was several times more expensive than the Dominican project's anticipated cost. In their own time, moreover, the two enterprises were intertwined and very much of a piece. Not only did they both develop during the 1850s and again after the Civil War, and share some of the same champions, they revealed a passion for territory and political expansion. Their advocates also promised greater national power and security, and they mentioned, though somewhat less frequently, the reported existence of gold fields in both places as well as other riches to be obtained—in Alaska from fish, furs, ice, and timber, or in Santo Domingo from coffee and sugar.

What really linked Alaska and the Dominican Republic in newspaper comments and in political discussion, however, were the allegations of lobbying and corruption in both cases. Reports of a Dominican "job" surfaced while Seward still held office and abounded *before* President Grant dispatched his first mission to the Dominican Republic. One reason for these developments is that the rumors of an Alaskan scandal, which metamorphosed into the snarled congressional investigation, heightened sensitivities about Dominican speculators. Reporters and editors sought new game, political alarms sounded, and deeper fears stirred; within months, the first major investigation of the Dominican enterprise was underway.

Historians who have played down or dismissed the murky issue of corruption have not only overlooked the resemblance and even some direct connections between the Alaskan and Dominican affairs, they have missed seeing the development of the pattern of late nineteenth-century American expansionism. Newspaper stories and the Alaska investigation left a taint on the Alaska purchase and made it seem, at least to some persons, a seriously dishonest deal; while the acquisition was an accomplished fact, expansionism generally encountered new skepticism. When charges were levelled against the Dominican project, suspicions of expansionism spread. For the next twenty-five years, expansionism was widely, though by no means uniformly, associated with corruption. Expansionist projects accordingly suffered frustration on these grounds.

Such was the fate of Grant's Samoan designs in the mid-1870s. The president had approached this project with caution, largely because of the embarrassments he had suffered over Santo Domingo and because of congressional opposition; but the South Seas expeditions of his commissioner and old comrade in arms, Colonel Albert B. Steinberger, while officially limited, possessed considerable expansionist potential. Alas for its promoters, the Samoan adventure not only encountered British opposition, it became associated — far-fetched as this may seem to historians who have not explored the issue of political corruption — with the sensational St. Louis Whisky Ring and District of Columbia Safe Burglary Conspiracy Cases. The link between distant Samoa and scandals in Washington, as any reader of the contemporary press was aware, was the President's personal secretary, General Orville Babcock, who had first attained notoriety in the extended Dominican controversy and now was forced to give up his position with Grant.[6]

The more ambitious Hawaiian ventures during the administration of Benjamin Harrison met the same fate. By this time, the

Alaska scandal had been forgotten, but veteran reporters and editors quickly revived memories of the Dominican scandal.[7] Meanwhile, new accusations raised by the press and by various interested parties involved everything from the alleged machinations of the "Sugar Trust" and "Sugar King" Claus Spreckels to reports of an Opium Ring and a lottery, and the revival of native witchcraft and immoral hulas.[8] This exotic mixture, poured into an already bubbling domestic political pot, resulted in too strong a brew to win American approval.

Only in 1898 was there a break in the pattern of expansion blocked owing to cries of corruption, because, on this occasion, the administration's opponents were themselves expansionists, and no scandal materialized. President William McKinley's chief critics in Congress — Populists, Bryan Democrats, and Silver Republicans — favored Cuban independence, which some of them saw as the first step toward the island's inevitable assimilation by the United States. They accused McKinley of opposing independence for Cuba and charged that the President was conspiring with foreign bondholders who allegedly possessed a vested interest in retention of the island by Spain. The accusations were groundless. Nevertheless, on the eve of war, such suspicions took peculiar forms, notably the Teller amendment, whose real purpose — textbook explanations to the contrary — was to avoid any United States responsibility for the so-called Cuban debt.[9] The Silver Republicans, and some Democrats and Populists, continued to advocate expansion, as well as to distrust the President even when, after war came, he pursued some of the goals they favored in foreign policy. In the end, McKinley, with consummate political skill, accomplished what no previous President or secretary of state — not even the relentless Grant or the cagey Seward — had been able to do: annex Caribbean and Pacific islands.[10]

The story of the failure of expansion in Santo Domingo, Samoa, and Hawaii, and of the successes of 1898, and the vital if difficult task of probing allegations of dishonesty in each case, will require another volume. The significant Dominican story is especially tangled and overlain with misleading innuendoes and historical myths. But one revealing aspect of the Dominican affair, a torrent of charges of corruption involving Santo Domingo during and as a result of the Alaska investigation, can be described succinctly. This account will also help to complete the story of the Alaska scandal and its impact.

There were connections between Alaska and Santo Domingo —
some political and personal, others involving the spirit and ideas
of expansion — as far back as the 1850s. For the most part, each enterprise went on its own way, but, after the Civil War, they occasionally became intertwined again. The summer of 1868, before the
Alaska scandal broke, is a suitable moment to pick up the story.
On July 1, the advocates of Alaska tested sentiment for passage of
the appropriation bill. Banks and Stevens spoke at some length on
behalf of Alaska, and the press covered the debate in detail. The
New York Herald, which favored passage, featured Stevens's arguments in one article, reporting that, if there was anything for which
he gave Seward credit, it was his effort at expansion, and that he
would have forgiven the secretary all his sins if Seward also had
persisted in acquiring Samaná Bay in the Dominican Republic![11]

Johnson, Seward, Banks, Walker, and other prominent political
figures shared Stevens's ambitions. One of the last gasps of such explicit dual expansionism — the linking of Alaskan and Caribbean
acquisitions — came on December 9, 1868, five months after Stevens's
speech. In his annual message, President Johnson referred to the
purchase of Alaska as having been "made with the view of extending national jurisdiction and republican principles in the American
hemisphere." In his very next sentence he called for "a further step,"
the addition of the islands of St. Thomas and St. John. He then
urged "the acquisition and incorporation into our Federal Union
of the several adjacent continental and insular communities as speed-
ily as it can be done peacefully." The President referred both to
the islands of Santo Domingo and Cuba, but he emphasized the
"annexation of the two Republics of the island of St. Domingo."[12]
Already made unlikely by his administration's extreme unpopularity,
Johnson and Seward's expansionist hopes were doomed by the break-
ing Alaska scandal. Indeed, on the very day of the President's message, metropolitan papers reprinted the *Worcester Spy's* revelations
about corruption in the Alaska purchase, and members of the House
of Representatives scrambled to establish a formal investigation.

Champions of Dominican projects thereafter usually avoided or
played down references to Alaska, or tried to distinguish between
the ventures. An ironical instance occurred on February 9, 1869.
Just one day after its reporter, Uriah Painter, was grilled for the
third time by the congressional committee looking into the Alaska
scandal, the *New York Sun*, which had approved the purchase with

some reluctance but seldom belabored it, advocated the acquisition of Santo Domingo. It reasoned that there were only 100,000 inhabitants on the island and that the land was valuable compared to Alaska![13]

Opponents of Dominican ventures, both under Johnson and Grant, had an easier time of it. They tried to establish a connection to the Alaska affair, even when the link was tenuous, or simply damned one project by mentioning the other. Newspapers that were themselves accused of complicity in the Alaska scandal had to treat this matter carefully. In an editorial of January 14, 1869, early during the congressional investigation, the *New York Tribune* struck a blow at expansion north and south but avoided any direct reference to the current scandal, then receiving so much attention in the press: "An exceedingly important and valuable part of the duty of a legislative body is the prevention of legislation. The House took up this part of its duties yesterday, and discharged it well. The plan of [Banks] for saddling us with a protectorate of Hayti and Santo Domingo was ably debated and peremptorily killed." Greeley added gratuitously, in a slap at the purchase, which his paper had never favored but which was now causing unanticipated difficulties, "And the ludicrous formality of a territorial Government for our icebergs and Esquimaux was done to death with almost equal emphasis. It was a good day's work."[14]

The task of smearing the Dominican project with the crime of Alaska was simpler for newspapers such as the *New York Herald*, which had somehow itself escaped accusation and which was one of the chief purveyors of insinuations about payoffs. The *Herald*, which had the largest circulation of any American newspaper, was more responsible than any other paper for initiating stories about Dominican as about Alaskan scandals. It began to attack Dominican projects as corrupt during the first days of the Alaska investigation and kept up this refrain throughout the inquiry. The influence of the Alaska scandal on the paper can be seen by comparing its treatment of Dominican annexation before and after the opening of the Alaska investigation. Some months earlier, in January 1868, the *Herald* published several stories about modest Dominican and American expansionist ideas, such as the proposed lease of a naval base, but treated them routinely.[15] President Johnson's proposals for annexation of the island, made in December 1868, elicited strong opposition from the paper. The *Herald* at once condemned this idea and blamed Seward for it, remarking sarcastically, "It is what we might have suspected from a head so full of annexation projects." The editor's objections were based largely on racial prejudice, however, as had been characteristic of the paper's attacks on the Johnson administration: "The addition to the Union of a State entirely made up of niggers, tame and wild, about half and half . . . an out-and-out experiment of negro supremacy is a stunner."[16] The next day's editorial was in the same vein: "To annex St. Domingo is to add to our troubles and increase our population by half a million of negroes educated to revolutionary turmoil."[17]

Five days later, on December 16, as the Alaska investigation heard its first witnesses, the *Herald* reported that New York capitalists had secured a perpetual lease of Samaná Bay and that the United States would proceed to establish a naval station. Other newspapers quickly picked up this incomplete and inaccurate story. The editor of the *San Francisco Alta California*, which had been one of the first papers to raise questions about corruption in the Alaska purchase, complained on December 17: "The Samaná Bay purchase, or lease, turns out to be very much like a job." He speculated, without any firm evidence, that "a company of New York capitalists — the Alta Vela Association, perhaps — " lay behind the operation.[18]

As the Alaska investigation wound on, the *Herald*'s own coverage of Dominican matters abandoned racial themes and concentrated on the richer issue of corruption. During early January 1869, the paper ran a half-dozen such stories and editorials with increasingly serious allegations. On January 8, 1869, for instance, a *Herald* dispatch from Washington reported that "Colonel [Joseph] Fabens, of Greytown, American West Indian Company, and San Domingo Company notoriety is here, in connection with the project to purchase the Bay of Samaná." The allusions to Fabens's background, which most informed readers of the paper would have understood, were to the American entrepreneur's ties to the regime of filibusterer William Walker in Nicaragua and to an ill-fated wartime undertaking, of which Fabens was secretary and to which President Abraham Lincoln had given encouragement, to settle Black Americans in the Dominican Republic. (Most of the ill-prepared and unfortunate settlers became sick, or died, or went home.[19]) On the next day, the *Herald* published a long story, bitterly prejudiced against Fabens and his associates, to the effect that the present effort was "to deceive the American people and get money from them," that it was "unlawful," and that it was "only a job."[20]

A *Herald* editorial of January 14 recalled Fabens's previous activities but specified new charges. The occasion for the comment was Banks's proposal for a Dominican protectorate, which that government's agent favored: "We suppose this means Mr. Fabens, whose career as Finance Minister for Walker in Nicaragua and sundry other little things some years ago will be remembered. This gentleman has a Samaná bay plot [of land] and some little steamship plans to help President [Buenaventura] Baez"[21] Over the next eighteen months, these charges about holdings of Dominican real estate and commercial franchises circulated ever more widely and were steadily embellished, until Senator Charles Sumner himself stated that Fabens, presidential secretary Babcock, and even Grant held property on Samaná Bay.[22] The accusations about Babcock and Grant created a storm in the Senate and brought to a head the bitter struggle over the President's annexation proposal. Sumner's charges, which were broadcast by papers hostile to the administration, doomed Grant's effort to revive annexation and cost the Senator his chairmanship of the Foreign Relations Committee. The shock waves continued into 1872, as some Republicans bolted their party in consequence of the Dominican affair.[23]

All of this lay far in the future in early 1869, when the *New York Herald* drummed away on the refrain of corruption in the Johnson administration. In some editions, the *Herald* accused rival newspapers of involvement in the Alaska scandal; at other times, it condemned Dominican projects as speculations. Within one period of ten days, beginning in late January 1869, the paper ran six stories and editorials about Santo Domingo. On occasion it mixed in a racial slur, but financial wrongdoing was the main theme.[24]

Other newspapers and magazines gradually took up the scent. On February 1, the *Washington National Republican* sniped at "St. Domingo, by Jingo."[25] "Rumor prevails," it was reported in the *Washington Daily Morning Chronicle* on February 10, "that the scheme for the annexation of San Domingo is a huge job intended to benefit almost solely certain parties who have obtained grants of nearly the whole territory of the island." The *Baltimore Sun* quoted "an eminent lawyer" who was preparing an "exposé of the project, and declares that it is merely a scheme to enable certain parties to get control of the Bay of Samaná and certain guano deposits."[26]

The Nation joined the attack, somewhat belatedly, on February 11: "The St. Domingo annexation scheme, as we feared, is likely to come up again. . . . If the United States Government, therefore, engages in any such transaction . . . it will become a party to a wretched little fraud, and an unprofitable one besides. . . . those who do not want to see the army increased, a leak of unknown magnitude opened in the Treasury, and a ring formed beside which the Whiskey Ring and the Indian Ring would fade into insignificance, ought to protest against it with all their might."[27] Reformer E.L. Godkin's magazine would, a year later, become one of the most persistent critics of Grant's Dominican project.[28]

For the moment, however, *The Nation*, the *New York Herald*, and other papers that criticized Dominican proposals, reduced their fire. The Johnson administration was coming to an end, and it was obvious that the President and Seward would not attain their ambitions. In mid-February, the attention of the press returned to the Alaska investigation, and there was impatient speculation about the committee's findings. When the report was at last made public, a flurry of stories and editorials appeared, with the *New York Herald*, as usual, providing the most extended coverage and commentary.[29] Then, as noted before, the attention of the press turned to the new Grant administration.

During the next nine months, throughout the remainder of 1869, many stories appeared in the press about the interest of the President in Santo Domingo, and there was extensive coverage of the special mission he sent to the island. But commentary was restrained, and Grant carefully attempted to avoid the slightest hint of corruption by employing as his emissary General Babcock, his able wartime aide-de-camp and trusted presidential secretary. The country was weary from the bitter controversies of the Johnson years, moreover, and the press gave his administration the benefit of the doubt. Democratic politicians launched periodic sallies, but Grant enjoyed widespread respect and had many staunch defenders. As late as January 6, 1870, *The Nation* denounced a "scandalous and utterly unpardonable attack on the executive" by such critics.[30]

But then the President's good fortune ran out. As he prepared to seek Senate approval of his Dominican ventures, it became apparent that the press and Congress had not, after all, forgotten the

Alaska scandal. In a report of January 12, 1870 — some nine months after the Alaska investigation ended — the *New York Herald* revived fears of new frauds and memories of the earlier controversy: "A rumor has been started that certain worthies have succeeded in negotiating a loan of some millions of dollars to the Dominican government since the arrangement of the treaty [negotiated by General Babcock]. . . . This fact has been brought to the attention of the House Committee on Foreign Affairs. . . . It is feared that some scoundrels . . . have set up a job, to use a lobby expression. The Committee will thoroughly investigate this matter, and though they are in favor of the provisions of the treaty they are determined that there shall be no stealing fund, as appeared in the Alaska purchase."[31]

A few days later, on January 17, the *New York Times* ran a lengthy article supporting the plan of the Grant administration to annex the Dominican Republic. The writer attacked efforts "in certain quarters to convey false information to the people" and asserted that "probably no subject of this kind was ever effected with a clearer record than this." The reporter continued defensively: ". . . what disgusts the newspaper and Congressional lobby here is the fact that the project seems likely to go through, as a significant measure of the Administration policy in the West Indies, without even the meagre dripplings of the Alaska case."[32] The *Times* was shouting into the wind, for widespread if not always warranted suspicions remained that there had been corruption in the purchase of Alaska. The paper's seeming confidence in Grant's project would prove mistaken, too.

Within a few days after the President and General Babcock took the Dominican treaties to Senator Sumner, the old charges of corruption reappeared. The *New York Tribune*, for example, wrote of the effort of "unscrupulous parties" to "swindle our Government."[33] By early February, *The Nation* had joined the outcry against "the St. Domingo Bargain."[34] Complaints followed quickly that Joseph Fabens and his friends had conspired with Dominican authorities to imprison another American, one Davis Hatch, so that he would not interfere with the annexation deal. On February 21, the Senate called upon the Department of State for all the papers involving Hatch, and Grant complied promptly.[35] A major congressional investigation followed, featuring the familiar allegations of financial corruption involving Fabens and his associates but pursuing these charges in great detail. There were accusations, too, that Babcock had exceeded his authority and abused power. The episode, which received extensive press coverage, undoubtedly damaged the chances for Grant's treaties. The majority report, issued just before the Senate voted on annexation, rejected Hatch's petition, but an accompanying minority report severely castigated Fabens, Babcock, and other agents of the administration.[36]

As the Dominican affair developed its own momentum and became a major political issue, Alaska faded from public attention. But the earlier scandal had left its mark on the mind of the day, and opponents of the administration continued to exploit this memory. During another heated phase of the prolonged Dominican battle, in January 1871, the *Washington Daily Patriot*, a newly established Democratic newspaper that had attacked Grant relentlessly from its very first edition, invoked the negative images of Alaska: "Presses subsidized by Federal patronage, or influenced by the promise of reward, as they were in the case of Alaska, have feebly attempted to uphold the fraud. But they signally failed to make the least impression on the country, or even to qualify the general conviction that the [Dominican] scheme is steeped in corruption, and is a monstrous collusion to obtain money by fraudulent pretenses, contrived by venal speculators in New York, Boston, and Washington."[37] Thus the Alaska affair again was put to political use in the Dominican controversy, for editors and congressmen recognized its symbolic importance. Because of its impact on the dramatic, influential Dominican scandal, as well as because of its own implications for expansionism, the Alaska scandal had more lasting impact on American foreign relations than historians have recognized.

Even in the early twentieth century, when the importance of these events had passed and the public's memory had faded, some officials still recalled fragments of the controversies. "Whenever there has been a sudden revelation of sporadic wrongdoing in the Philippines, or allegations of wrongdoing in connection with our foreign policy," President Theodore Roosevelt wrote to Secretary of State John Hay in 1902, "a perfect crop of people has arisen whose attitude was as unreasonable as that of Horace Greely [sic] himself."[38]

Two tasks remain before this account of the Alaska scandal can be closed. The first is to offer some general observations on why expansionism became associated with corruption and accordingly suffered frustration; the second, which will be addressed in the appendix that follows, is to review some of the specific charges of dishonesty.

Difficult as it may be for later generations nurtured on anti-imperialism and anti-expansionism to accept, expansionism after the Civil War was strongly moral and idealistic. Pride in the United States and a desire to extend the power of the nation permeated expansionist thought; genuine belief in the benevolence of American expansion accompanied such views. But these very ideals posed a threat to expansionism, for even the slightest hint of corruption called the entire effort in doubt.

As mentioned at the beginning of the essay, Americans historically have been a suspicious lot, with a talent for finding abuses in government. Expansionist projects were especially susceptible to suspicion because a second major ingredient, or motivation, was economic — chiefly the desire for more land and resources, such as timber, minerals, fish, or tropical products, but sometimes also for trade. Thus American expansionism bore the seeds of its own destruction. For the very existence of the desire for profit and economic advantage raised doubts in the minds of others about who would gain from a particular project. So long as the proposal was discussed in the abstract, or in terms of national advantage, the debate in Congress was straightforward, if sometimes heated, and the decision made on its merits, even if sometimes wrongly evaluated. Once the issue of a lobby or of special interests was raised, however, the project came in jeopardy. At the same time, only the persuasion of lobbyists such as Robert J. Walker and Frederick Stanton and the force of special interests such as the Russian government or of Joseph Fabens and his friends could maintain the steady pressure required to move the project through Congress. Given a free, competitive, and suspicious press, as was the case after 1865, and a Congress that responded, though sometimes grudgingly, to newspaper revelations, suspicion of scandal was inevitable.

When one scandal occurred, the search by the press and by Congress for other crimes intensified; and the receptivity to allegations increased. In the case of expansionism, evidence sufficient to create suspicion was easy to find. This did not mean evidence sufficient to convict, for the newspaper and congressional investigations were not nearly so rigorous as a court of law presumably should be. As is suggested in the appendix, moreover, charges levelled by contem-

poraries and by later historians against individual figures in the
Alaska affair are subject to considerable question; some of those
accused appear to have been innocent. But, at the time, the accusers only needed to find enough evidence, or to invent it, in order
to write a striking story or editorial and to make a political point.

The purchase of Alaska survived the scandal because of its timing. That deed was done. Expansionists with equally reputable
motives — those who wanted to acquire the Dominican Republic —
faced a greater obstacle because they had to overcome the presump-
tion of dishonest dealings. The challenge proved too great even for
Grant, the wartime hero, in large part because the suspicions ante-
dated his project. What the President had envisaged as a popular,
easy accomplishment became a serious political defeat and personal
ordeal. Grant's congressional supporters, in fact, had to seek vindication of his reputation by establishing a special commission after
encountering renewed opposition to annexation. (The President won
immediate praise for his selection of a distinguished and impartial
panel: Ben Wade, former president of the Senate; Andrew Dexter
White, the president of Cornell University; and Samuel Gridley
Howe, the prominent reformer and friend of Senator Sumner. Frederick Douglass, the nation's leading Black citizen, was named secretary.)[39] When the commissioners reported, Grant transmitted the
document to Congress with a message revealing not only that the
charges of corruption had hurt him deeply but that, in his view,
they had come to overshadow the original issue of annexation: "The
mere rejection by the Senate of a treaty negotiated by the President
only indicates a difference of opinion between two coordinate de-
partments of the Government, without touching the character or
wounding the pride of either. But when such rejection takes place
simultaneously with charges openly of corruption on the part of
the President or those employed by him the case is different. Indeed, in such case the honor of the nation demands investigation.
This has been accomplished by the report of the commissioners here-
with transmitted, and which fully vindicates the purity of the motives and action of those who represented the United States in the
negotiation. And now my task is finished."[40]

Grant's official vindication notwithstanding, suspicions of corruption remained, and expansionist projects suffered from the taint.
When rumors of corruption surfaced again during the Samoan affair five years later, expansionism was dealt another sharp blow.

Not until the Hawaiian Revolution of 1893 did territorial expansionism revive from the setbacks under Grant; and then, once more, the pattern of allegations and frustration recurred.

Despite their faith that destiny was manifestly on their side, the expansionists of the Gilded Age suffered one rebuff after another. Their problem was not just bad luck or poor timing, but rather that the first scandal — the Alaska affair — fed other suspicions and that opportunistic journalists and politicians then attacked expansionist enterprises against which allegations had been made. Suspicion is one of the dominant political attitudes in the United States, and the nation's public affairs are notably sensitive to startling revelations and to implications of wrongdoing. The messy and contentious American system of politics often frustrates policies derived from ideas and interests. Without a doubt, this pattern of public behavior, which sometimes operates to the nation's loss and occasionally to its gain, remains very much alive today.

APPENDIX: WAS BANKS BRIBED?

By the early twentieth century, the once-famous Alaska scandal was largely forgotten — overshadowed by later, more sensational affairs. Interest revived in 1912, when William A. Dunning, an authority on politics during the era of Reconstruction, published an article featuring an unusual manuscript, dated September 6, 1868, that he had found in the papers of Andrew Johnson. In this scrawled memorandum, quoted in its entirety earlier, President Johnson recorded Secretary Seward's revelation to him that Minister Stoeckl secured passage of the Alaska appropriation bill by paying $30,000 to John W. Forney, $20,000 to Robert J. Walker and his associate Frederick P. Stanton, $10,000 to Representative Thaddeus Stevens, and $8,000 to Representative Nathaniel P. Banks.[1]

Since 1912, many books and articles have repeated the allegations in Johnson's memorandum. Some writers have expanded, or qualified, or denied them. I have earlier mentioned John Bigelow's account, which cannot be verified, asserting that Seward possessed the money intended for Stevens, and explained why it was likely that Stoeckl himself made off with the lion's share. In this appendix I shall summarize opinion about payments to the first four men named in the President's memorandum and focus at greater length on the issue of whether Banks was bribed.

There can be no doubt that Stoeckl rewarded John W. Forney's newspapers. Only the sum remains in doubt. Johnson put down a figure of $30,000 for Forney, while Walker, as described before, testified to the congressional investigating committee that Forney's brother was given $3,000 for the articles run in their papers. Walker stated, moreover, that Stoeckl had employed him as counsel for a total compensation of $26,000 gold, of which he gave $5,000 in currency to Stanton.[2] We have found that Stanton also was a go-between for the Russian minister and newspapermen other than the Forneys.

The case of Stevens, one of two public officials incriminated in the memorandum, is quite another matter. Even the cynical Dunning, who disliked Radical Republicans and once described Stevens as truculent, vindictive, and unscrupulous, was skeptical that old Thad had received a share of the Alaska payments because of his illness during the summer of 1868 and his death on August 11.[3] Historian Benjamin P. Thomas, whose work appeared in 1930, took the position that direct evidence for a payment to Stevens was lacking, that Stevens was friendly to Seward and to his policies, and that Stevens's action on the related issue of the Perkins claim was correct and might well have been taken on principle.[4] Two biographers of Stevens also vigorously defended him. Ralph Korngold pointed out that Stevens on another occasion had rejected an offer of money.[5] Fawn Brodie argued that Stevens's established position on Alaska and his death in August made a Russian payment to him unlikely.[6] Historian Robert Ferrell weighed the contradictory evidence in 1975 and questioned whether the payment to Stevens took place.[7] It is possible, nevertheless, that Stoeckl bribed Stevens or, more likely, that the exuberant envoy simply meant to reward him after passage of the appropriation. There was time enough for the payment to have been arranged. As for Stevens, he engaged in other large financial transactions and clearly was concerned about his worldly estate during the last weeks of his life.[8] Yet, the circumstances, the thinness of evidence, and Stevens's steadfast support of expansion so far have won a verdict of not guilty from most scholars.[9]

Nathaniel Banks has not fared so well. At first glance, it is difficult to understand why historians and biographers have treated the attractive, articulate Banks more harshly than the grim and often virulent Stevens. Both men were of very humble New England origins. Stevens, the crippled son of an impoverished cobbler, became a highly successful lawyer in Pennsylvania before going to the state legislature and to Congress, acquired extensive real property, and built a large ironworks. Banks, who left school to labor as a bobbin boy in a textile mill, also became a lawyer, won election to the Massachusetts legislature and then to the House of Representatives (where he was Speaker during 1856–1857), served a term as governor of Massachusetts, and just prior to the Civil War assumed the position of resident director in Chicago of the Illinois Central Railroad. Stevens was too old for military service and remained in Congress during the war, while President Lincoln appointed Banks a major general of Union volunteers. By 1865, Banks was commanding officer of the Gulf Department. When his pursuit of Lincoln's conciliatory policies stirred the opposition of radicals, Banks left military service and ran successfully for the House of Representatives from Massachusetts again.

The different historical images of Stevens and Banks resulted essentially from their postures on reconstruction. Old Thad, champion of Negro rights and unrelenting enemy of President Johnson, embodied Radical Republicanism. General Banks was a moderate. He did favor Negro suffrage and voted for impeachment but he strongly disliked Senator Charles Sumner and felt uncomfortable with the views of other New England Radicals.[10] Banks's horizons were broadening, moreover, and his interests shifted to foreign policy.

There was little to distinguish Banks and Stevens, however, on postwar issues of territorial expansion. Chairman Banks of the Foreign Affairs Committee and Chairman Stevens of the Appropriations Committee led the fight for the Alaska bill. They also strongly supported Seward's ideas about the Dominican Republic.[11] As for Russian bribes, historian Dunning, who essentially acquitted Stevens, suggested that Banks was implicated but escaped inquiry owing to the stratagems of protective congressional colleagues.[12] Several other historians of the affair likewise have treated Banks as guilty.[13]

Banks's most severe critic was historian Fred Harvey Harrington. Harrington did concede that Banks had turned down "bribes" during his service in New Orleans and was determined to win passage of the Alaska bill. But such arguments — which Stevens's biographers deemed sufficient to acquit him — did not impress Harrington, who concluded that Stoeckl already possessed the support that he paid Banks for! Harrington meanwhile contended in a brief but sharp indictment that Banks took gifts from businessmen, was hard-pressed by debts, did not earn enough as a congressman to pay his expenses, and wanted to visit Europe with his family. Besides, Harrington argued, Banks himself stated that "frauds are inseparable from all matters connected with the Government." Harrington la-

ter repeated his charge, adding that Banks "succumbed to tempta-
tion" even after helping to secure a pay increase for Congress in
1866.[14]

Any defender of Banks would need to examine Harrington's
sources, which were chiefly the Banks papers, or find new evidence.
It is difficult to check the citations, however, for the bulk of the
Banks correspondence, located in the Essex Institute in Salem, Massachusetts when Harrington used this material, was subsequently
transferred to the Library of Congress and combined with other
Banks materials. Perhaps some items were lost in the process; in
any event, approximately one-fourth of the letters Harrington cited
to support the passages summarized above are not to be located
in the Banks papers in the Library of Congress. For example, a letter dated January 1, 1867, from R.E. Robbins of the American Watch
Company, which Harrington mentioned twice to prove that a businessman sent a check to Banks, does exist; but the two other letters
that Harrington mentioned in the same footnote are missing.[15] A
few of Harrington's citations, moreover, are incorrectly dated, perhaps as a result of typographical errors.

Some of the Banks letters that can be found have been used out
of proper time context or do not seem quite to support Harrington's
argument. For instance, Harrington cited newspapers of 1854 and
1856 when discussing Banks's views on political ethics in 1866 and
1867.[16] Again, Banks's letter to his wife on January 16, 1863, cannot
be found; but there is a long letter from Banks in occupied New
Orleans to his wife and to his mother on January 15, 1863. It does
not, however, refer very clearly to offers of "bribes" but rather (to
his wife) disclaims any interest "in plunder" and (to his mother)
complains that "every body connected with the government has been
employed in stealing other people's property."[17]

The citations are even more troublesome for Harrington's asser-
tion that Banks faced pressing debts as a congressman, lacked income to cover his congressional expenses, wanted to visit Europe,
and hence took Stoeckl's bribe. The first letter that Harrington cited
is dated March 26, 1864, four years earlier, when Banks was still
in the army. The second letter, dated September 7, 1865, was written the day after Banks received his army discharge and slightly
more than one month *before* he was nominated for Congress. In
the third letter, dated November 22, 1867, Banks told his wife, who
had remained in Waltham, that he had taken

winter quarters on the corner of 15th & G Streets, in the high brick building on G St., next to the Conservatory or flower House, if you remember it, and opposite the Treasury Building. Two finely furnished rooms for $70 per month — a Restaurant or Cook Shop under the building kept by a cold woman will furnish my breakfast & perhaps my dinner in my room. There will be room for a Lady bye and bye. Kiss the darling children for me . . .[18]

There is no mention in the letter of financial problems.

The combined Banks manuscripts in the Library of Congress, on the other hand, contain some revealing information that Harrington did not cite. These items included Banks's diaries, with his income and personal expenses listed for some months in 1867, 1868, and 1873, and letters exchanged by Banks and his wife during the family's travels and his own tour in 1869. Quite a clear picture of the Banks's finances can be established. In January 1867, the worst month recorded, Banks received a congressional salary of $400 and spent $440, but that included a payment of $128 in taxes, probably for his farm property and city lots in Massachusetts.[19] In March 1868 he spent $86 for room and board, gave his wife $59, and had other minor expenses, for a total of $215. In May 1868 he laid out $109 for room and board, had other cash expenses of $9, and gave Mrs. Banks $35, for a total of $153, which meant that he saved $247.[20]

Mrs. Banks and their children went to Europe in late 1868 or early 1869. Banks allegedly had received Stoeckl's bribe payment of $8,000 before this time. If so, the new wealth did not appear in the family's finances. Banks at first doled out money to his wife in bills of exchange of about $100 a month, then had the sergeant-at-arms of the House of Representatives send $200 monthly from his salary. On one occasion Banks chided his wife gently about an account she had run up at Stewart's in New York City before her departure, explained that he had paid the bill, and said that was why he could not send so much that month.[21]

One of Mrs. Banks's letters to her husband spoke of seeking "cheap accommodations" in Milan and of barely having enough money to get there.[22] Later she wrote of receiving £36 but wishing she had $400 a month, "if you had the means," because they "were entirely without money."[23] Again, in 1871, she reported expenses for board of $25 each month.[24] Numerous other letters from Banks and his wife throughout this period were in the same vein. The family was able to travel. Occasionally Mrs. Banks splurged, as when she spent

$350.40 one day in Paris.[25] But generally the expenditures were modest.

Banks, moreover, did not have to rely solely on his congressional salary. Their farm began to show a profit by the summer of 1869, and their city lots in Waltham rose sharply in value.[26] Soon after telling his wife of this good news and of even better future prospects for the city property, Banks himself travelled to Paris, Stockholm, and St. Petersburg. He notified the sergeant-at-arms regularly on all drafts that were to be paid, and this official remitted funds as required.[27]

The junket may have been partly at government expense, for Banks inspected various canals and locks in Europe. It was essentially a private undertaking, however, for Banks was involved in a venture to construct a Darien canal. His associates included Massachusetts businessman Nathan Appleton, who was his travelling companion and delegate of the Boston Board of Trade to the inaugural of the Suez Canal, C.B. Norton, and other American and European investors. (The project collapsed in February 1870.)[28] In Paris, moreover, as Banks later informed his wife, Baron Rothschild had asked him to undertake some "legitimate business."[29]

Banks's visit to St. Petersburg, however, was the high point of the trip. During the battle over Alaska, he had openly expressed his ambition to become minister to Russia. He had not achieved that aim, but now he was able to accompany the new American minister. They were received cordially, and Banks participated in an imperial review of troops.[30] If Stoeckl had bought him off in 1868, however, the Russian government must not have been pleased when Banks pressed the Perkins claims again during his visit.[31]

During the next year, 1870, the Waltham farm continued to do fairly well, and Banks sent a larger check of $300 to his wife.[32] By 1873 the general developed still another source of income, as he received numerous fees of $75 and $100 for lectures and other appearances.[33]

Nathaniel Banks on occasion accepted a financial contribution from a business constituent. So far as a bribe for the Alaska bill is concerned, the surviving evidence suggests that the verdict should be not guilty, or at least not proven.

NOTES

Introduction

1. Oliver M. Dickerson, *The Navigation Acts and the American Revolution* (Philadelphia: Univ. of Pennsylvania Press, 1951); Edmund S. Morgan, *The Birth of the Republic, 1763–89* (Chicago: Univ. of Chicago Press, 1956); Bernard Bailyn, *The Ideological Origins of the American Revolution* (Cambridge: Harvard Univ. Press, 1967), a masterful, if somewhat contradictory, book.

2. Among the landmarks in this ongoing debate are Charles A. Beard, *An Economic Interpretation of the Constitution of the United States* (New York: Macmillan, 1913), and Forrest McDonald, *We the People: The Economic Origins of the Constitution* (Chicago: Univ. of Chicago Press, 1958).

3. An introduction to the Yazoo affair may be obtained from Irving Brant, *James Madison, Secretary of State, 1800–1809* (Indianapolis: Bobbs-Merrill, 1953), 234–40, 433–59; Marshall Smelser, *The Democratic Republic, 1801–1815* (New York: Harper, 1968), 135–36, 181–83; Norman Risjord, *The Old Republicans: Southern Conservatives in the Age of Jefferson* (New York: Columbia Univ. Press, 1965), ch. III; Dumas Malone, *Jefferson the President: First Term, 1801–1805* (Boston: Little, Brown, 1970), 246–47, 448–57.

4. Leonard White, *The Jacksonians: A Study in Administrative History, 1829–1861* (New York: Macmillan, 1954), 424–28; Edward Pessen, "Corruption and the Politics of Pragmatism: Reflections on the Jacksonian Era," in Abraham S. Eisenstadt, Ari Hoogenboom, and Hans L. Trefousse, eds., *Before Watergate: Problems of Corruption in American Society* (New York: Columbia Univ. Press, 1979), 79–98.

5. Ari Hoogenboom, "Civil Service Reform and Public Morality," in H. Wayne Morgan, ed., *The Gilded Age* (rev. ed., Syracuse: Syracuse Univ. Press, 1970), 77–95. The first five pages of this chapter comprise by far the most perceptive and balanced commentary on the extent and meaning of corruption and allegations of official dishonesty during the Gilded Age.

6. Louis Filler, *Crusaders for American Liberalism: The Story of the Muckrakers* (Yellow Springs, Ohio: Antioch Press, 1964). Later books such as Matthew Josephson, *The Politicos, 1865–1896* (New York: Harcourt, Brace, 1938), were very much in the muckraking tradition. Zane L. Miller, *The Urbanization of Modern America: A Brief History* (New York: Har-

court, Brace, 1973), cites a number of recent scholarly urban histories and biographies that deal in part with political machines and corruption. Eric L. McKitrick, "The Study of Corruption," *Political Science Quarterly*, 72 (Dec. 1957), 502–15. There was also the work of such political scientists as Harold Gosnell, V.O. Key, and, more recently, Arnold Heidenheimer. See also the chapter by Ari Hoogenboom cited in note 5 above.

7. C. Vann Woodward, ed., *Responses of the Presidents to Charges of Misconduct* (New York: Dell, 1974).

8. Morton Keller, *Affairs of State: Public Life in Late Nineteenth Century America* (Cambridge: Harvard Univ. Press, 1977), 238–58, 524–43; "Corruption in America: Continuity and Change," in Eisenstadt et al., *Before Watergate*, 7–19.

9. Arthur M. Schlesinger, Jr., and Roger Bruns, eds., *Congress Investigates: A Documented History, 1792–1974*, 5 vols. (New York: Chelsea House, 1975). The editors did not include the Alaska investigation in their impressive compilation.

10. J. Martin Klotsche, "The Star Route Cases," *Mississippi Valley Historical Review*, XXII (Dec. 1936), 407–18; Lucius E. Guese, "St. Louis and the Great Whiskey Ring," *Missouri Historical Review*, XXXVI (Jan. 1942), 168–83; J. Leonard Bates, *The Origins of Teapot Dome* (Urbana: Univ. of Illinois Press, 1963); Burl Noggle, *Teapot Dome: Oil and Politics in the 1920s* (Baton Rouge: Louisiana State Univ. Press, 1962). See also Robert K. Murray, *The Harding Era: Warren G. Harding and His Administration* (Minneapolis: Univ. of Minnesota Press, 1969).

11. For further discussion, see Ch. 1. The first note in that chapter contains bibliographical references.

12. Recent expressions of this view include D.P. Crook, *Diplomacy During the American Civil War* (New York: Wiley, 1975), 191–92; Robert E. May, "Lobbyists for Commercial Empire: Jane Cazneau, William Cazneau, and U.S. Caribbean Policy, 1846–1878," *Pacific Historical Review*, XLVIII (Aug. 1979), 383–84.

13. Notable among the many publications in this vein are the books by two presidents of the American Historical Association: Samuel Flagg Bemis, *The Latin American Policy of the United States* (New York: Norton, 1943), and *American Foreign Policy and the Blessings of Liberty and Other Essays* (New Haven: Yale Univ. Press, 1962); Dexter Perkins, *The Evolution of American Foreign Policy* (New York: Oxford Univ. Press, 1948, 1966), and *The American Approach to Foreign Policy* (Cambridge: Harvard Univ. Press, 1962).

14. The leading revisionist works are William Appleman Williams, *The Tragedy of American Diplomacy* (New York: Dell, 1959, 1962), and *The Roots of the Modern American Empire: A Study of the Growth and Shaping of Social Consciousness in a Marketplace Society* (New York: Knopf, 1969); Walter La Feber, *The New Empire: An Interpretation of American Expansion, 1860–1898* (Ithaca: Cornell Univ. Press, 1963); Thomas J. McCormick, *China Market: America's Quest for Informal Empire, 1893–1901* (Chicago: Quadrangle, 1967); Kenneth J. Hagan, *American Gunboat Diplomacy and the Old Navy, 1877–1889* (Westport: Greenwood, 1973);

Ernest N. Paolino, *The Foundations of the American Empire: William Henry Seward and U.S. Foreign Policy* (Ithaca: Cornell Univ. Press, 1973). Criticisms of this "open-door" interpretation appear in Paul A. Varg, "The Myth of the China Market, 1890–1914," *American Historical Review* LXXIII (Feb. 1968), 742–58; Paul S. Holbo, "Economics, Emotion, and Expansion: An Emerging Foreign Policy," in H. Wayne Morgan, ed., *The Gilded Age*, rev. ed. (Syracuse: Syracuse Univ. Press, 1970), 199–221; J.A. Thompson, "William Appleman Williams and the 'American Empire,'" *Journal of American Studies*, VII (April 1973), 91–104; Robert L. Beisner, *From the Old Diplomacy to the New, 1865–1900* (New York: Crowell, 1975), esp. 18–28. Charles S. Campbell, *The Transformation of American Foreign Relations, 1865–1900* (New York: Harper, 1976), is a balanced treatment that restores some of the emphasis on expansion.

CH. 1 "THE ACQUISITION OF ALASKA"

1. These works include J.M. Callahan, *The Alaska Purchase and Americo-Canadian Relations* (Morgantown: Univ. of West Virginia Press, 1908); Frank A. Golder, "The Purchase of Alaska," *The American Historical Review*, XXV (April 1920), No. 3, 411–25; Benjamin Platt Thomas, *Russo-American Relations, 1815–1867* (Baltimore: Johns Hopkins Univ. Press, 1930), pp. 143–66; Hallie M. McPherson, "The Interest of William McKendree Gwin in the Purchase of Alaska, 1854–1861," *The Pacific Historical Review*, III (March 1934), No. 1, 28–38; Thomas A. Bailey, "Why the United States Purchased Alaska," ibid., 39–49; Victor John Farrar, *The Annexation of Russian America to the United States* (Washington, D.C.: W.F. Roberts Co., 1937); Virginia H. Reid, *The Purchase of Alaska: Contemporary Opinion* (Long Beach: Press-Telegram, 1939); Anatole G. Mazour, "The Prelude to Russia's Departure from America," *The Pacific Historical Review*, X (Sept. 1941), No. 3, 311–19; David Hunter Miller, "The Alaska Treaty," unpublished manuscript, The National Archives, c. 1942–44, Microcopy No. T–1024; Richard E. Welch, Jr., "American Public Opinion and the Purchase of Russian America," *American Slavic and East European Review*, XVII (1958), 481–94; Hector Chevigny, *Russian America: The Great Alaskan Venture, 1741–1867* (New York: Viking Press, 1965); Glyndon G. Van Deusen, *William Henry Seward* (New York: Oxford Univ. Press, 1967), esp. 535–49; Ernest Paolino, *The Foundations of the American Empire: William H. Seward and United States Foreign Policy* (Ithaca: Cornell Univ. Press, 1973); Howard I. Kushner, *Conflict on the Northwest Coast: American-Russian Rivalry in the Pacific Northwest, 1790–1867* (Westport, Conn.: Greenwood, 1975); Ronald J. Jensen, *The Alaska Purchase and Russian-American Relations* (Seattle: Univ. of Washington Press, 1975), a judicious and comprehensive study.

2. See especially William A. Dunning, "Paying for Alaska," *Political Science Quarterly*, XXVII (Sept. 1912), 385–98; Reinhard H. Luthin, "The

Sale of Alaska," *The Slavonic (and East European) Review*, XVI (July 1937), 168–82; Jensen, *The Alaska Purchase*, 122–32; and the works by Thomas, Farrar, and Miller cited in note 1, Ch. 1.

3. House of Representatives, 40th Congress, 3d Session, Report No. 35, February 27, 1869, pp. 11–12; hereafter cited as "Alaska Investigation." Reinhard H. Luthin has argued that there is little evidence to support Walker's claim, which he considers suspect under the circumstances, "The Sale of Alaska," 168–69. See also Miller, "The Alaska Treaty," 56–64, and Jensen, *The Alaska Purchase*, 3, 143. Walker, an unrelenting expansionist, had made a similar claim in a newspaper letter and pamphlet issued early in 1868, well before the scandal broke; *The Daily Morning Chronicle* (Washington, D.C.), Jan. 30, 1868. James P. Shenton accepts Walker's contention in his biography, *Robert John Walker: A Politician from Jackson to Lincoln* (New York: Columbia Univ. Press, 1961), 210–11.

4. Jensen, *The Alaska Purchase*, 4–9, 17–20; Golder, "The Purchase of Alaska," 411; McPherson, "The Interest of William McKendree Gwin," 33–35; Thomas, *Russo-American Relations*, 145–46.

5. "Alaska Investigation," 19; Clay to Seward, May 10, 1867, in U.S. House Executive Documents, 40th Congress, 2d Session, Vol. 13, Ex. Doc. No. 177, p. 12; Van Deusen, *William Henry Seward*, 539; Jensen, *The Alaska Purchase*, 38; H. Edward Richardson, *Cassius Marcellus Clay: Firebrand of Freedom* (Lexington: Univ. of Kentucky Press, 1976), 95–96.

6. Frederick W. Seward, *Seward at Washington as Senator and Secretary of State* (New York: Derby and Miller, 1891), III, 346. See also Paolino, *Foundations*, and Kushner, *Conflict*, esp. 106–13, 154, for the emphasis on trade, especially with the Pacific and Asia. Jensen, *The Alaska Purchase*, 62–67, is a good summary of specific issues and larger factors moving Seward. I am indebted to Kinley J. Brauer for discussion of Seward's views.

7. Jensen, *The Alaska Purchase*, 7–8, 9–10; Kushner, *Conflict*, 133–36; Golder, "The Purchase of Alaska," 411–12; Mazour, "The Prelude to Russia's Departure," 311–15. Mazour and others have established that Russia's asirations reached their zenith in 1821, when Alexander I issued a ukase proclaiming ownership of the Pacific coast to 51°, or Vancouver Island, and forbidding all foreigners to fish or trade within 100 miles of the coast. In 1824 Russia and the United States signed a convention limiting Russia's claims to 54°40′; in 1825 England negotiated a similar agreement.

8. Mazour, "The Prelude to Russia's Departure," 316; Golder, "The Purchase of Alaska," 413; Constantin to Gorchakov, March 22/April 3, 1857, copy, Manuscripts Division, Library of Congress, I-9, No.4; Jensen, *The Alaska Purchase*, 15, 20; Kushner, *Conflict*, 134, 138–39.

9. Mazour, "The Prelude to Russia's Departure," 316–17; Jensen, *The Alaska Purchase*, 5, 13, 16; Kushner, *Conflict*, 136–37; Golder, "The Purchase of Alaska," 413–15; Van Deusen, *William Henry Seward*, 537.

10. Thomas, *Russo-American Relations*, 146–47; Golder, "The Purchase of Alaska," 414–16; McPherson, "The Interest of William McKendree Gwin," 35–37; Jensen, *The Alaska Purchase*, 14–23, 47–49; Kushner, *Conflict*, 136–37.

11. Golder, "The Purchase of Alaska," 417; Mazour, "The Prelude to Russia's Departure," 312, 315, 317–18; Thomas, *Russo-American Relations*, 145; Kushner, *Conflict*, 139–40.

12. Van Deusen, *William Henry Seward*, 539; Jensen, *The Alaska Purchase*, 24–34.

13. Golder, "The Purchase of Alaska," 417–19; Jensen, *The Alaska Purchase*, 51–61; Kushner, *Conflict*, 141.

14. Van Deusen, *William Henry Seward*, 540; Jensen, *The Alaska Purchase*, 69–70; Kushner, *Conflict*, 141.

15. Golder, "The Purchase of Alaska," 419; Jensen, *The Alaska Purchase*, 70–71; *Memoirs of Cornelius Cole: Ex-Senator of the United States from California* (New York: McLoughlin, 1908), 281–83. Cole represented San Francisco interests headed by Louis Goldstone, Port Collector John F. Miller, and Judge E. Burke, the senator's brother-in-law. With State Department approval, he wrote Minister Clay on behalf of the enterprise but received a discouraging reply on Feb. 1, 1867. Curiously, Stoeckl, on returning to Washington, at first spoke so encouragingly that Cole informed the company that the matter was settled in their favor; then Stoeckl told him that the Californians would have to be disappointed and "offered to palliate matters." Cole expressed no objection to the sale though it did not favor his constituents. The Washington Territory petition of January 1866, which was widely publicized after the treaty was negotiated, is printed in U.S. House Executive Documents, 40th Congress, 2d Session, Vol. 13, Ex. Doc. No. 177, pp. 4–5. Jensen, *The Alaska Purchase*, 44–45, revealed the private interests behind the Washington Territory's petition, which Seward employed to reopen the issue of Russian America. Richardson, *Cassius Marcellus Clay*, 96–97, has confirmed the minister's support of Alaskan projects. See also Kushner, *Conflict*, 131–32.

16. Jensen, *The Alaska Purchase*, 71–74; Kushner, *Conflict*, 143–44; Van Deusen, *William Henry Seward*, 540–41; *Diary of Gideon Welles: Secretary of the Navy Under Lincoln and Johnson*, ed. Howard K. Beale and Allen Brownsword (New York: Norton, 1960), III, 66. *The Diary of Orville H. Browning*, ed. James G. Randall, Vol. 22, *Illinois Historical Collections*, p. 137; U.S. House Executive Documents, 40th Congress, 2d Session, Vol. 13, Ex. Doc. No. 177, pp. 10–11; Golder, "The Purchase of Alaska," 419–20; Thomas, *Russo-American Relations*, 151, said $10 million, as did Frederick Seward, *Seward at Washington*, III, 347; Frederic Bancroft, *The Life of William H. Seward* (New York: Harper, 1900), II, 475–77.

17. Frederick Seward, *Seward at Washington*, III, 348; Van Deusen, *William Henry Seward*, 541; Bancroft, *The Life of William H. Seward*, II, 477; David Donald, *Charles Sumner and the Rights of Man* (New York: Knopf, 1970), 303–4; Jensen, *The Alaska Purchase*, 75–78.

18. Donald, *Sumner*, 304n, and others point out that Emanuel Leutze's famous painting of the signing incorrectly shows Sumner present. The artist's license seems justified.

19. *San Francisco Alta California*, April 2, 3, 1867. Other reports of an initial negative Senate response are to be found in the *New York Herald*, and the *Philadelphia Press*, April 2, 1867. Welles, *Diary*, III, 75; Donald,

Sumner, 305–6; Golder, "The Purchase of Alaska," 420; Van Deusen, *William Henry Seward*, 541–43, pointed out that Stoeckl was prepared to blame Seward if the treaty failed.

20. See, for instance, the *New York Herald*, April 9, 1867. My examination of a dozen papers, largely on the two coasts, confirms the findings of Reid, Bailey, and Kushner about the press's reactions. Many papers also carried State Department information about the petition of the Washington territorial legislature; e.g., *Washington Evening Star*, *New York Tribune*, April 1, 1867.

21. See, for instance, the *New York Sun*, *New York Herald*, April 6; *Washington Daily Morning Chronicle*, April 6, 9, 11; *Washington Daily National Intelligencer*, April 6, 1867.

22. Donald, *Sumner*, 306–7.

23. Ibid., 307–10; U.S. House Executive Documents, 40th Congress, 2d Session, Vol. 13, Ex. Doc. No. 177, pp. 124–361, esp. 143. Jensen, *The Alaska Purchase*, 83–92, described the committee's divisions and Sumner's speech.

24. Golder, "The Purchase of Alaska," 421; Stoeckl, who did little for the treaty's passage, blamed the Americans for its minor deficiencies, Jensen, *The Alaska Purchase*, 93–95.

25. U.S. House Executive Documents, 40th Congress, 2d Session, Vol. 13, Ex. Doc. No. 177, pp. 13–21; Thomas, *Russo-American Relations*, 154; Jensen, *The Alaska Purchase*, 100–1.

26. Golder, "The Purchase of Alaska," 421; Van Deusen, *William Henry Seward*, 544–45; Jensen, *The Alaska Purchase*, 87. On Stevens's views, see *Washington Daily Morning Chronicle*, April 11, 1867.

27. Van Deusen, *William Henry Seward*, 543; *New York Sun*, April 2, also 1, 10, 1867.

28. *New York Tribune*, April 1, 6, 8, 9, 1867; Bernard A. Weisberger, "Horace Greeley: Reformer as Republican," *Civil War History*, 23 (March 1977), 5–25.

29. *New York Herald*, *New York World*, April 9, 1867. For representative reactions to these threats, see *Washington Daily National Intelligencer*, April 9, 1867, which that day suggested that Alaska's ice be traded for "tropical products"; also see the *Washington National Republican*, April 10, 13, 1867.

30. *Philadelphia Inquirer*, April 1, 1867; *Daily Alta California*, April 2, 1867; *New York World*, April 2, 1867.

31. *New York Tribune*, April 8, 9, 1867; *New York Herald*, April 9, 1867.

32. *New York Tribune*, April 10, 1867.

33. Bancroft, *The Life of William H. Seward*, II, 481–83; Charles C. Tansill, *The Purchase of the Danish West Indies* (Baltimore: Johns Hopkins Univ. Press, 1932), 5–61.

34. Brainerd Dyer, "Robert J. Walker on Acquiring Greenland and Iceland," *Mississippi Valley Historical Review*, XXVII (Sept. 1940), 263–64; Van Deusen, *William Henry Seward*, 531–32.

35. James D. Richardson, *A Compilation of the Messages and Papers of the Presidents*, VI, 524.

36. Miller, "The Alaska Treaty," 429; *Congressional Globe*, 40–1 (July 17, 1867), 675.

37. There is no definitive study of the claim. The fullest account is Miller's unpublished manuscript, "The Alaska Treaty," 428–503, but it is necessary to consult many other works, including Van Deusen, *William Henry Seward*, 538, 545; Golder, "The Purchase of Alaska," 422; Farrar, *The Annexation of Russian America*, 85–86; Thomas, *Russo-American Relations*, 155; Luthin, "The Sale of Alaska," 170; Jensen, *The Alaska Treaty*, 98–99; Fred H. Harrington, *Fighting Politician: Major General N.P. Banks* (Philadelphia: Univ. of Pennsylvania Press, 1948), 182. Simon Stevens had been involved during the Civil War in scandalous munitions deals, Fawn M. Brodie, *Thaddeus Stevens* (New York: Norton, 1966), 95–96.

38. Thomas, *Russo-American Relations*, 155; U.S. House Executive Documents, 40th Congress, 2d Session, Vol. 13, Ex. Doc. No. 177, p. 21; Jensen, *The Alaska Treaty*, 99.

39. *Congressional Globe*, 40–1 (Nov. 25, 1867), 792–93; *House Journal*, 40th Congress, 1st Session, 266–67.

40. U.S. House Executive Documents, 40th Congress, 2d Session, Vol. 13, Ex. Doc. No. 177, p. 21.

41. Richardson, *Messages*, VI, 580. Seward probably drafted the message.

42. Golder, "The Purchase of Alaska," 422–23.

43. *Congressional Globe*, 40–2 (Dec. 9, 1867), 92–95.

44. Ibid. (Dec. 11, 1867), 135; U.S. House Executive Documents, 40th Congress, 2d Session, Vol. 13, Ex. Doc. No. 177.

45. *Congressional Globe*, 40–2 (Jan. 7, 1868), 371.

46. Ibid. (Feb. 10, 1868), 1092.

47. Ibid. (March 6, 1868), 1706–7.

48. *Washington Daily Morning Chronicle*, Jan. 25, 28, 29, 30, 1868, April 3, 9, 11, 1867. On the Walker-Forney friendship, ibid., Nov. 12, 1869. The *Chronicle* advocated the acquisition of the Danish islands on March 21, 1868. The paper was filled with material advocating impeachment from March to May 1868. Forney's resignation was traceable to senatorial politics and the defalcation of a clerk, whose shortages Forney made good; this matter also figured in the later scandal. Forney had offered to resign in May, but the Senate laid his offer on the table at the time.

49. *New York Times*, Feb. 10, 1868; "Alaska Investigation," 10–12. The *Chronicle* reported brisk "public demand" and from February 10 to March 13 advertised the pamphlet at five cents a copy.

50. Tansill, *Danish West Indies*, 126–27; Luthin, "The Sale of Alaska," 171. A pedantic footnote is required at this point to determine whether Walker began his paid lobbying by January 1868, as Luthin avers, or in late spring, as Walker told the House investigating committee. The questions of motive and money are at issue. Luthin, citing letters from Walker to Washington banker W.W. Corcoran of April 16 and 30, 1867 (Corcoran Papers, Library of Congress), argued that Walker's distressed financial condition — including the prospect of forced sale of his Washington estate, "Woodley," under a legal judgment, and the illness of a daughter — made him receptive to Stoeckl's approach and set him at work by January. No

such letters can be found in the Corcoran Papers today, and the Manuscript Division's old card index suggests that no letters with such dates were ever on deposit there. Luthin may simply be the victim of a typographical error, for Walker did write his friend Corcoran (who had retired from banking) regarding "Woodley" on April 9, while ten months later, on February 25, 1868, following the death of Corcoran's daughter, Walker confided that his own daughter was very ill with consumption and required treatment. The letter of April 9 is in the Library of Congress Corcoran Papers, and the second appears in Corcoran's memoirs, *A Grandfather's Legacy* (Washington: Polkinhorne, 1874), p. 268, neither of which Luthin cites. Miller, "The Alaska Treaty," 513 fn., which was prepared shortly after Luthin wrote, checked Luthin's sources, found the April 9 letter and corrected Luthin's argument by noting that Walker's financial troubles were "earlier, in April 1867, when Walker asked Corcoran for help which was granted." Miller also cited as evidence another letter, of August 7, 1868, also in the Library of Congress Corcoran Papers, and the memoirs, in which Walker told Corcoran that his help the previous year had been "the turning point financially." Miller's research is impeccable and his conclusion sound. The illness of Walker's daughter in February 1868, moreover, could have had little bearing on the expansionist letters that Walker composed in January 1868. Other small errors in this portion of Luthin's narrative require that it be used with care. I conclude that Walker testified accurately when he stated that Stoeckl engaged him in May as counsel. Similar reasoning based on different evidence appears in Miller, "The Alaska Treaty," 515. Jensen, *The Alaska Purchase*, 110-11, also says May but does not develop the point. Details of Walker's financial situation can be found in Shenton, *Walker*, 177-78, 208-12, but this book is inaccurate in finding Walker's financial status unimproved in 1868. There is only a passing comment in Henry Cohen, *Business and Politics in America from the Age of Jackson to the Civil War: The Career Biography of W.W. Corcoran* (Westport, Conn.: Greenwood, 1971), 216, but this book is valuable on the earlier close financial connections between Corcoran and Walker.

51. Shenton, *Walker*, 212, 269; Tansill, *Danish West Indies*, 126; "Alaska Investigation," 11.

52. *Washington Daily Morning Chronicle*, Jan. 28, 29, 30, 1868; "Alaska Investigation," 11.

53. Stoeckl to Banks, Jan. 5, 1868, Box 69, Banks Mss., LC.

54. Boston lawyer Dwight Foster, counsel for Mrs. Perkins, appealed to Banks on behalf of that "lady of intelligence and worth," left in "extreme poverty" because Russia had broken the contract, Foster to Banks, March 4, 1868, Box 71, Banks Mss., LC. A clergyman and constituent from Everett counseled Banks that "*We owe Russia*" and must pay even for a "bad bargain," Rev. I.F. Holton to Banks, March 1868, Box 71, Banks Mss., LC.

55. Miller, "The Alaska Treaty," 438.

56. *Congressional Globe*, 40-2 (March 14, 1868), 1870-75.

57. *New York Herald, Washington Daily Morning Chronicle, New York Tribune*, March 19, 1868.

58. Banks to Seward, Dept. of State, Misc. Letters, March 20, 1868, part 2; Miller, "The Alaska Treaty," 441.

59. Seward to Stoeckl, March 23, 1868, Dept. of State, Six Notes to Russia, 241–42; Miller, "The Alaska Treaty," 442.

60. Golder, "The Purchase of Alaska," 423; Miller, "The Alaska Treaty," 442B; Jensen, *The Alaska Purchase*, 108–9.

61. Golder, "The Purchase of Alaska," 423–24.

62. "Alaska Investigation," 12, 19; James A. Rawley, *Race and Politics: "Bleeding Kansas" and the Coming of the Civil War* (Philadelphia: Lippincott, 1969), 214, 232, 249; Roy Nichols, *The Disruption of American Democracy* (New York: Free Press, 1967), 107–16, 159–60.

63. Nichols, *Disruption*, 59, 91, 179, 418–22, 427; "Alaska Investigation," 35; George Fort Milton, *The Age of Hate: Andrew Johnson and the Radicals* (New York: Coward-McCann, 1930), 533–34, 636; R.W. Latham to Samuel Tilden, July 13, 1868, Box 8, Tilden Mss., NYPL.

64. Charles H. Coleman, *The Election of 1868: The Democratic Effort to Regain Control* (New York: Columbia Univ. Press, 1933), 215; Walker to Tilden, May 30, 1868, Box 8, Tilden Mss., NYPL; Alexander C. Flick, *Samuel Jones Tilden: A Study in Political Sagacity* (New York: Dodd, Mead, 1939), 172.

65. *Washington Daily Morning Chronicle*, June 24, 27, 1868; "Alaska Investigation," 12.

66. *Washington Daily Morning Chronicle*, June 24, 27, 1868.

67. Ibid., July 9, 11, 13, 14, 1868.

68. Ibid., July 1, 1868; *New York Herald*, July 13, 1868; (Washington) *Daily National Intelligencer*, July 13, 1868. Even avowed opponents of Alaska, such as Elihu Washburne, received letters favorable to the territory; see J & W Seligman to Washburne, June 1868, Letterbook 60, Washburne Mss., LC.

69. *New York Sun*, June 29, 1868. Painter wrote on June 27.

70. Banks to Seward, June 27, 1868, folio 154, Seward Mss.; Miller, "The Alaska Treaty," 452.

71. *Congressional Globe*, 40–2 (June 27, 1868), 3556.

72. Ibid., Vol. 84 (June 30, 1868), Appendix, 385–92. The *New York Times*, July 2, 1868, properly criticized his excessive claims for Russia's friendship.

73. *Congressional Globe*, Vol. 84 (June 30, 1868), Appendix, 392–400; *New York Sun*, June 29, 1868.

74. Luthin, "The Sale of Alaska," 174–75.

75. Ibid. See also "Alaska Investigation," 18, 35, 39.

76. The best analysis of lobbying during the early Gilded Age is to be found in an unpublished paper by Margaret Thompson Echols, "Priorities and Legislative Politics: Agenda-Setting in the Reconstruction Congress," meeting of the Organization of American Historians, Boston, April 1975. F.C. Grey (of the *Washington Daily Morning Chronicle*) to Ben Butler, March 28, 1870, Box 50, Butler Mss., LC, revealed prejudice against Painter but also made clear his important role and the extent of lobbying by journalists.

77. H.D. Cooke to Painter, March 2, 1868; Thomas A. Scott to Painter, Feb. 28, Dec. 7, 8, 1868, Jan. 20, 1869; W.A. Harding to Painter, July 9, 1868; I.W. England to Painter, Dec. 1, 1870; Oakes Ames to Painter, June 23, 25, 1871; Painter financial statement, Dec. 31, 1868, all in Box 116-C, Painter Mss., Historical Society of Pennsylvania; Ellis Paxson Oberholtzer, *Jay Cooke: Financier of the Civil War* (Philadelphia: George Jacobs, 1907), II, 91, 111, 335, 342, contains other details of Painter's lobbying for Cooke's railroad and insurance interests between 1867 and 1872.

78. Roscoe Conkling to Painter, May 13, 1869; Ben Wade to Painter, May 17, 1869; Galusha Grow to Painter, Sept. 21, Nov. 18, Dec. 19, 1868; Painter to William E. Chandler, Sept. 20, 1869, all in Box 116-C, Painter Mss., HSP; "Alaska Investigation," 33.

79. Charles A. Dana to Painter, March 31, June 5, 23, 1868, Box 116-C, Painter Mss., HSP.

80. *New York Sun*, July 10, Sept. 25, 1868.

81. I.W. England to Painter, July 17, 1868, Box 116-C, Painter Mss., HSP.

82. *New York Sun*, April 1, 1867; "Alaska Investigation," 35.

83. *New York Sun*, April 1, 2, 10, 1867.

84. Ibid., April 15, 1867; June 30, 1868.

85. Ibid., June 29, 1868; "Alaska Investigation," 39.

86. *New York Sun*, July 1, 1868.

87. Shenton, *Walker*, 213; Jensen, *The Alaska Purchase*, 113.

88. *New York Tribune*, July 6, 1868.

89. *New York Sun*, July 2, 8, 1868; *New York Tribune*, July 8, 10, 1868; W.B. Lawrence to Banks, July 13, 1868, Box 72, Banks Mss., LC.

90. G.W. Warren to Banks, July 11, 1868; Banks to Mrs. Banks, July 15, 1868, Box 72, Banks Mss., LC; an ordinary voter condemned the "reckless Squandring" (sic) by "dictators" Johnson and Seward, John Rees to Banks, July 6, 1868, ibid.

91. Benjamin F. Butler, *Butler's Book: Autobiography and Personal Reminiscences* (Boston: A.M. Thayer, 1892), 530; Hans L. Trefousse, *Ben Butler: The South Called Him Beast* (New York: Twayne, 1957), 210; *Congressional Globe*, 40–2 (July 7, 1868), 3810–11, Appendix 400-3.

92. *Congressional Globe*, 40–2 (July 14, 1868), 4053.

93. *New York Sun, Washington Evening Star*, July 15, 1868; *Congressional Globe*, 40–2 (July 14, 1868), 4055.

94. R.W. Latham to Samuel Tilden, July 13, 1868, Box 8, Tilden Mss., NYPL. The letter is printed in John Bigelow, ed., *Letters and Literary Memorials of Samuel J. Tilden* (New York: Harper & Brothers, 1908), I, 240, but this version contains a number of minor errors, and the editor has misidentified Latham as a congressman from California. Publication, however, probably preserved the original letter from destruction by Tilden's protective executors.

95. Coleman, *Election of 1868*, 300–1; Flick, *Tilden*, 181; Irving Katz, *August Belmont: A Political Biography* (New York: Columbia Univ. Press, 1968), 176–77. Katz's account contains a serious chronological error, and his own footnote does not support his claim that "Belmont rejected Latham's scheme." On Perrin, see Nichols, *Disruption*, 116.

96. R.W. Latham to Mr. Wood, July 20, 1868, Box 8, Horatio Seymour papers, New York State Library, Albany; Coleman, *Election of 1868,* 239–40, 249–50. For further information on Van Buren, who was not Martin Van Buren's son "Prince John," see ibid., 58, 82, 115–17, 123, 128–29, 136–37, 173, 183–84, 215–24; Bigelow, *Letters,* 202–3, 212; Flick, *Tilden,* 171–79; Stewart Mitchell, *Horatio Seymour of New York* (Cambridge: Harvard Univ. Press, 1938), 104, 300–1, 405–8, 439–41.

97. Banks to Mrs. Banks, July 15, 1868, Box 72, Banks Mss., LC; *Washington Evening Star,* July 14, 1868, confirmed that Banks received praise in Congress.

98. James G. Blaine, *Twenty Years of Congress* (Norwich: H. Bill, 1886), ii, 337; *New York Tribune,* July 18, 1868; *New York Sun,* July 20, 1868.

99. Blaine, *Twenty Years,* II, 337–38; Jensen, *The Alaska Purchase,* 120; *Congressional Globe,* 40–2 (July 22, 23, 1868), 4340, 4392–94; *New York Tribune,* July 24, 1868; *New York Sun,* July 23, 25, 1868.

100. *New York Tribune,* July 16, 1868; see also June 30, July 15; *New York Sun,* June 30, 1868; *New York Times,* July 1, 2 (with objections to blocking the appropriation in this way), July 15, 1868; the *New York Herald,* July 2, 1868, differed from the other papers.

101. *New York Tribune,* July 20, 1868; *Semi-Weekly Tribune,* July 24, 1868.

102. *Washington Evening Star,* July 30, 31, Aug. 1, 1868; *New York Times,* Aug. 2, 1868; *New York Sun,* Aug. 3, 1868. Secretary Bodisco waited at the Clarendon Hotel in New York City while the transaction was completed, *New York Times,* July 28, 1868.

103. *Washington Evening Star,* Aug. 4, 1868.

104. Golder, "The Purchase of Alaska," 424; Miller, "The Alaska Treaty," 505–6.

105. *New York Herald,* Nov. 1, 1868.

106. Walker to Corcoran, Aug. 7, 1868, Corcoran Mss., LC; he also warmly thanked Corcoran for his aid the previous year, as did Mary Walker on Oct. 18, 1868, in Corcoran, *A Grandfather's Legacy,* 290; *Washington Daily Morning Chronicle,* Oct. 9, 10, 12, 1868.

Ch. 2 "The Alaska Scandal"

1. *New York Herald,* Sept. 11, 1868.

2. Carl Sandburg, *Abraham Lincoln, The War Years* (New York: Dell Edition, 1960), 515–16.

3. *New York Herald,* Jan. 3, 1868.

4. *Washington Daily National Intelligencer,* March 18, 1868.

5. *Washington Weekly Chronicle,* March 7, 1868. Rollins himself was indicted in an early whisky-fraud case but acquitted.

6. Ibid., May 30, 1868; Brodie, *Stevens,* 355.

7. *Washington Evening Star,* July 3, 1868.

8. *New York Times*, July 28, 1868.

9. *New York Herald*, Feb. 3, 8, 1869; *New York World*, Feb. 10, 1869. The most useful source on its subject is *Trial of Andrew Johnson* (Washington, D.C.: Government Printing Office, 1868), II, 144–46, 260–68, 280–84, 307–8. Also useful were G.B. Van Deusen, *Thurlow Weed: Wizard of the Lobby* (Boston: Little, Brown, 1947), 330–34; Brodie, *Stevens*, 415; Lately Thomas, *The First President Johnson* (New York: Morrow, 1968), 583–84; David Miller Dewitt, *The Impeachment and Trial of Andrew Johnson* (New York: Russell, 1967), 397–401; Milton, *Age of Hate*, 534–38, 573–74.

10. Roy F. Nichols mentions Alta Vela in *Advance Agents of American Destiny* (Philadelphia: Univ. of Pennsylvania Press, 1956), 202–4; Charles C. Tansill, *The United States and Santo Domingo* (Baltimore: Johns Hopkins Univ. Press, 1938), 290–316; Kinley J. Brauer, "Gabriel Garcia y Tassara and the American Civil War: A Spanish Perspective," *Civil War History*, 21 (March 1975), 5–10; Milton, *Age of Hate*, 535; *Trial*, II, 144–45; Van Deusen, *Weed*, 331; Brodie, *Stevens*, 415.

11. Brodie, *Stevens*, 415; Milton, *Age of Hate*, 535; *Trial*, II, 144–45, 262–65; Dewitt, *Impeachment*, 398–99; Tansill, *The United States and Santo Domingo*, 312–16. The others were James A. Garfield of Ohio and James G. Blaine of Maine.

12. Dewitt, *Impeachment*, 400; *Trial*, II, 144–45; Tansill, *The United States and Santo Domingo* 316–20; Milton, *Age of Hate*, 536, 538; Brodie, *Stevens*, 415.

13. Van Deusen, *Weed*, 332–33; *Trial*, II, 144–46; Tansill, *The United States and Santo Domingo*, 320–26, harshly condemned Nelson's assertions.

14. *Trial*, II, 262–68, 280–84, 307; Brodie, *Stevens*, 415; Van Deusen, *Weed*, 332–33.

15. J.R. Young to E.B. Washburne, July 17, 1868, Letterbook 60, Washburne Mss., LC. There is a fine sketch of Young by John C. Broderick, "John Russell Young: The Internationalist as Librarian," *The Quarterly Journal of the Library of Congress*, 33 (April 1976), 116–49.

16. "Alaska Investigation," 34, 38–39. Parts of this testimony are separated by two days.

17. Ibid., 38, on Latham's acquaintance with Painter; 39, for Painter's account. Latham's version was nearly identical, 35.

18. Ibid., 22–23.

19. Ibid., 16–18.

20. Ibid., 37–38.

21. Ibid., 32–35, 38–41.

22. Sarah Wallace and Frances Gillespie, eds., *The Journal of Benjamin Moran, 1857–65* (Chicago: Univ. of Chicago Press, 1949), II, 1268; *New York Herald, World, Times, Washington Daily Morning Chronicle*, Aug. 27, 1868.

23. *New York Herald, World, Times, Washington Daily Morning Chronicle*, Aug. 27, 1868.

24. "Alaska Investigation," 35–36.

25. Ibid., 40.

26. Ibid., 23.

27. Luthin, "The Sale of Alaska," 177; Miller, "The Alaska Treaty," 516, but Miller incorrectly added that Walker was carrying "cash," supposedly to pay "another (or others)," 546–47. See also Farrar, *The Annexation of Russian America*, 97.

28. The New York papers carried lists of prominent visitors and their hotels; see, e.g., *New York Sun*, Aug. 15, 17, 1868; *New York Times*, Aug. 18, 20, 1868.

29. *New York Sun*, Aug. 15, 17, 1868; *New York Times*, Aug. 18, 20, 1868; *Congressional Globe*, 40–2 (July 14, 1868), 4055; *Biographical Directory of the American Congress* (Washington: GPO, 1961), 1485.

30. *New York World*, *New York Herald*, Aug. 27, 1868.

31. "Alaska Investigation," 23, 33.

32. *New York Times*, Dec. 14, 1868.

33. "Alaska Investigation," 33, 7.

34. Ibid., 33.

35. Ibid., 7, 8, 23. In all likelihood, the Ohio reference crept in because of a concurrent rumor about the Ohio Whisky Ring. There might also have been confusion with a former representative from Ohio, A.G. Riddle, who was interested in the Perkins claim.

36. Memorandum, Sept. 1868, Vol. 145, Andrew Johnson Mss., LC; Dunning, "Paying for Alaska," 385–86; Miller, "The Alaska Treaty," 519.

37. John Bigelow Diary, vol. April 10–Dec. 31, 1868, p. 53, Bigelow Papers, NYPL; see text with commentary in Miller, "The Alaska Treaty," 522–23.

38. Further discrepancies appear upon comparison of the Bigelow diary, which is now in the New York Public Library, with his often quoted memoirs, John Bigelow, *Retrospections of an Active Life*, IV, 1867–1871 (Garden City, N.Y.: Doubleday, Page, 1913), 216–17. Bigelow's son unfortunately rewrote important passages of the diary in preparing the *Retrospections*. He inaccurately cut Walker back to $2,000, awarded Stanton an excessive fee of $10,000, and gave Forney $20,000; he designated another $10,000 for only *two* members of Congress and but $1,000 for "poor Thad Stevens." This butchered version of the manuscript diary can be given little credence, as David Hunter Miller made clear in his unpublished study, "The Alaska Treaty," 522–24, in the National Archives. For a sensible commentary on Thaddeus Stevens's part in all this, see Ralph Korngold, *Thaddeus Stevens: A Being Darkly Wise and Rudely Great* (New York: Harcourt, Brace, 1955), 431–33.

39. Dunning, "Paying for Alaska," 385; William E. Dodd, *Robert J. Walker, Imperialist* (Chicago: Chicago Literary Club, 1914); Bigelow, *Retrospections*, IV, 216–17. The letter from Stoeckl to Seward is dated May 17, 1869, and is quoted in Miller, "The Alaska Treaty," 506.

40. Chandler to Washburne, Oct. 19, 1868, Letterbook 61, Elihu Washburne Mss., LC.

41. The paper disappeared in mid-1869, reappeared briefly as the Democratic *Intelligencer and Express* in September 1869 and died in early 1870.

42. "Alaska Investigation," 17, 26, 27, 32, 40.

43. Ibid., 26.
44. Painter to Butler, Nov. 27, 1868, Box 44, Butler Mss., LC; Painter crossed out Bodisco's name. Copy Butler to Painter, Dec. 4, 1868, Box 44, Butler Mss., LC.
45. *New York Sun*, Nov. 30, 1868.
46. Ibid.
47. Ibid., Dec. 7, 8, 1868.
48. *Worcester Daily Spy*, Dec. 7, 15, 1868; *Congressional Globe*, 40–2, Vol. 83 (July 14, 1868), 4055. See also the *Daily Spy*, July 2, 8, 14, 15, 1868, for the paper's moderate reports at the time of passage of the appropriation. The fact that the *Daily Spy* was published in Worcester, the home of the Perkins family, seems to have been a coincidence. The paper revealed no special interest in the Perkins claim and seldom mentioned it.
49. *Worcester Daily Spy*, Dec. 7, 1868. Hinton noted that Butler might move for a committee of investigation but preferred "some one else to do that work."
50. *New York Sun*, Dec. 9, 1868; *New York Times*, Dec. 14, 1868.
51. *New York Herald*, Dec. 11, 14, 1868.
52. *New York World*, Dec. 12, 13, 1868.
53. *New York Sun*, Dec. 14, 1868; Painter did not mention Martin by name but referred to "a young Georgian."
54. Ibid.
55. *New York Herald*, Dec. 15, 1868; Alexander B. Callow, Jr., *The Tweed Ring* (New York: Oxford Univ. Press, 1969), 18–19; "Alaska Investigation," 1; *New York Tribune, Washington Daily Morning Chronicle*, Dec. 15, 1868.
56. *New York Tribune, New York Herald*, Dec. 15, 1868.
57. *New York Tribune*, Dec. 14, 15, 1868; *New York Sun*, Dec. 15, 1868; *New York Herald*, Dec. 24, 1868; Claude Fuess, *The Life of Caleb Cushing* (Hamden: Archon Books, 1965), II, 301.
58. *New York Herald*, Dec. 15, 1868.
59. Van Deusen, *Weed*, 329–30; *Washington Evening Star*, July 9, 1868.

CH. 3 "THE ALASKA INVESTIGATION"

1. "Alaska Investigation," 6–7.
2. Ibid., 8–9.
3. *Washington Daily Morning Chronicle, Philadelphia Press, Worcester Daily Spy, Washington Daily National Intelligencer, Washington National Republican, New York Tribune*, Dec. 17, 1868; *Washington Evening Star*, Dec. 16, 1868, conceding that Stoeckl might be able to account for his expenditures if he were in the country and inclined to testify.
4. *New York Herald*, Dec. 17, 1868.
5. The committee heard testimony on Dec. 16–19, 1868, Jan. 7, 11, 22, 23, 26, 29, Feb. 3, 6, 8, 1869. At least fourteen witnesses testified publicly.

Historians uniformly have relied on the official report, "The Alaska Investigation," printed Feb. 27, 1869, without realizing that it omitted the testimony of two witnesses. It also scrambled the order of their appearance and must be checked against other evidence, including news reports.

6. "Alaska Investigation," 11–16; *Washington Evening Star*, December 17, 18, 1868; *Washington Daily Morning Chronicle, Washington National Republican, New York Herald, New York Times, New York World, New York Tribune*, Dec. 18, 1868.

7. See the above citations and "Alaska Investigation," 29–30; Milton, *Age of Hate*, 585.

8. "Alaska Investigation," 25–27; *Washington Evening Star, New York World, New York Herald, New York Tribune*, Dec. 19, 1868. Hinton identified Martin as "George," which was incorrect. Shaw was a reporter-lobbyist.

9. "Alaska Investigation," 9–11, emphasis added; *Washington Daily Morning Chronicle*, Dec. 22, 1868; *Philadelphia Press*, Dec. 21, 1868; *New York World*, Dec. 22, 1868; *New York Herald*, Dec. 20, 1868; *Washington National Republican, New York Sun, New York Tribune*, Dec. 21, 1868; Dunning, "Paying for Alaska," 396–97.

10. *Washington Daily National Intelligencer*, Dec. 21, 1868; *New York Herald*, Dec. 20, 1868; Miller, "The Alaska Treaty," 509.

11. *New York Sun*, Dec. 22, 1868.

12. "Alaska Investigation," 19–21.

13. R.W. Latham to Samuel Tilden, July 13, 1868, Box 8, Tilden Mss., NYPL.

14. "Alaska Investigation," 27–29; *Washington Daily National Intelligencer*, Dec. 21, 1868; *Washington Evening Star*, Dec. 19, 1868; *New York World, New York Herald*, Dec. 20; *New York Sun*, Dec. 21, 1868, with greater detail on Noah; *New York Tribune*, Dec. 21, 1868.

15. "Alaska Investigation," 30–31; *Washington Daily National Intelligencer*, Dec. 21, 1868; *Washington Evening Star*, Dec. 19, 1868.

16. "Alaska Investigation," 32–35; *New York World, Sun, Herald, Tribune, Philadelphia Press*, Jan. 8, 1869.

17. "Alaska Investigation," 21–22; *New York Herald*, Jan. 9, 12, 1869; *New York World, Tribune, Sun*, Jan. 12, 1869; *Washington Evening Star*, Dec. 26, 1868.

18. *Washington National Republican*, Jan. 13, 1869; *New York Tribune*, Jan. 8, 1869; *New York Herald*, Jan. 8, 9, 1869; *New York Sun*, Jan. 9, 1869.

19. *New York Herald*, Jan. 12, 15, 22, 1869; *Washington National Republican*, Jan. 22, 1869.

20. *New York World, Tribune, Herald, Washington National Republican*, Jan. 23, 1869.

21. *New York Herald*, Jan. 27, 1869; *The Expositor* (Dec. 8, 1838–June 15, 1839); *Random shots and southern breezes* (2 vols., New York: Harper, 1842); *Woman: her character, her position, and her treatment* (Baltimore, 1850); *Morrison's strangers guide for Washington city* (Washington: O.H. Morrison, 1866); *Etiquette of Washington* (Washington: O.H. Morrison, 1866); *Washington Evening Star*, Jan. 28, 1869; *Philadelphia Press*, Jan.

29, 1869; Judge N.S. Howe to Nathaniel Banks, Jan. 29, 1869, Box 75, Banks Mss., LC; J.B. Stewart to Lewis Dent, March 2, 1870, Vol. 68, Hamilton Fish Mss., LC; unsigned letter, March 8, 1870, Hamilton Fish Mss., LC; Hamilton Fish Diary, Dec. 1, 1870, Vol. 2, Box 311, Fish Mss., LC: *New York Sun*, Jan. 27, 1869.

22. *New York Herald*, Jan. 27, 1869; *Washington National Republican*, Jan. 28, 1869; *New York Tribune*, Jan. 27, 1869; *New York Sun*, Jan. 27, 1869, claiming that it was Bodisco, not Stoeckl; *Washington Evening Star*, Jan. 28, 1869.

23. *New York Tribune*, Jan. 27, 1869; *Washington National Republican*, Jan. 28, 1869; Judge N.S. Howe to Nathaniel Banks, Jan. 29, 1869, Box 75, Banks Mss., LC.

24. "Alaska Investigation," 32; Nichols, *Disruption*, 72, 103, 157–58, 191–93, 210–18, 249–50, 285, 329, 421, 468; Painter earlier had reported that a subpoena had been issued to Wendell, *New York Sun*, Dec. 18, 1868; see also *New York Times*, Dec. 18, 1868. On Wendell's earlier scrapes, see Roger A. Bruns, "The Covode Committee, 1860," in Arthur M. Schlesinger, Jr., and Roger A. Bruns, eds., *Congress Investigates: A Documentary History, 1792–1974* (5 vols., New York: Chelsea House, 1975), II, 1068–1194, esp. 1073–80, 1092–1104.

25. "Alaska Investigation," 16–19; *New York Tribune*, Jan. 30, 1869. Este was a reporter-lobbyist.

26. "Alaska Investigation," 22–25; *Washington Evening Star*, Feb. 1, 1869; *Philadelphia Press*, Feb. 2, 5, 1869; *New York Herald*, Feb. 4, 7, 1869; *Washington National Republican*, Feb. 4, 5, 1869; *New York Tribune*, Feb. 4, 1869; *Washington Daily National Intelligencer*, Feb. 6, 1869.

27. *New York Herald*, Feb. 5, 7, 1869; *Washington National Republican*, Feb. 5, 6, 1869.

28. *Washington Evening Star*, Feb. 1, 1869; *Washington National Republican*, *New York Herald*, *New York Tribune*, Feb. 5, 1869; *New York Sun*, Feb. 8, 1869; his testimony is not printed in "Alaska Investigation;" W.W. Harding to U.H. Painter, telegram, Feb. 5, 1869, Box 116-C, Painter Mss., Historical Society of Pennsylvania.

29. *New York Tribune*, Feb. 4, 5, 8, 1869; *New York Sun*, Feb. 8, 1869.

30. *New York Tribune*, Feb. 8, 1869; *New York Herald*, Feb. 7, 1869.

31. W.W. Harding to U.H. Painter, telegrams, Feb. 5, 6, 7 (two), 1869, Box 116-C, Painter Mss., Historical Society of Pennsylvania.

32. "Alaska Investigation," 35–38; *New York Tribune*, Sun, Feb. 8, 1869.

33. *New York Sun*, Feb. 8, 1869.

34. Ibid., Feb. 9, 1869.

35. "Alaska Investigation," 38–41.

36. Ibid.

37. Ibid.

38. Ibid.

39. *Washington Daily Morning Chronicle*, Dec. 15, 17, 18, 22, 1868, when coverage ceased; Forney's *Weekly Chronicle* carried only one brief story, Dec. 26, 1868; *Worcester Daily Spy*, Dec. 15, 17, 19, 21, 1868; *San Francisco Alta California*, Dec. 28, 30, 1868, Feb. 18, 1869.

40. See, e.g., *New York Semi-Weekly Tribune*, Dec. 25, 29, 1868.

41. *Washington National Republican, New York Tribune, New York Herald*, Dec. 21, 1868.

42. J.R. Young to E.B. Washburne, Jan. 5, 1869; Henry Hilton to Washburne, Jan. 8, 1869, Letterbook 63, Elihu Washburne Mss., LC.

43. *New York Herald*, Jan. 22, 1869; *New York Tribune*, Feb. 2, 1869; *Washington Evening Star*, Feb. 8, 1869; *Washington Daily Morning Chronicle*, Feb. 9, 1869; see also *Washington National Republican*, Jan. 22, Feb. 4, 8, 1869.

44. *New York World*, Jan. 8, 1869; *Philadelphia Press*, Feb. 6, 1869.

45. *Washington Daily Morning Chronicle*, Dec. 19, 1868; *Philadelphia Press*, Jan. 8, Feb. 5, 6, 1869; the *Press* also attacked Tasistro, Jan. 29, 1869.

46. *San Francisco Alta California*, Dec. 28, 1868; *New York World*, Dec. 19, 1868; *New York Herald*, Dec. 20, 1868, Jan. 8, 1869; *New York Tribune*, Dec. 19, 1868, Feb. 8, 1869.

47. *Washington National Republican*, Dec. 17, 19, 1868, Feb. 4, 1869; *New York Herald*, Dec. 19, 1868.

48. *Washington Evening Star*, Dec. 18, 26, 1868; *New York Herald*, Dec. 18, 1868.

49. *Washington Evening Star*, Feb. 1, 1869; *New York Sun*, Feb. 8, 1869.

50. *New York Sun*, Dec. 18, 19, 21, 1868; see also Dec. 22, 1868, and subsequent issues.

51. *New York World*, Dec. 21, 22, 1868.

52. *New York Tribune*, Dec. 18, 1868, Jan. 19, 23, 30, Feb. 8, 1869; *New York Semi-Weekly Tribune*, Dec. 25, 1868.

53. *Washington Evening Star*, Feb. 8, 1869; *New York Times*, Dec. 8, 1868, Feb. 10, 1869.

54. *New York Tribune*, Feb. 10, 1869.

55. *New York Sun*, Feb. 11, 1869. The *Sun's* idea that Alaska be made a Siberia or Botany Bay gained widespread advocacy in the 1870s and 1880s, owing to continuing social problems in the United States and slow economic development in Alaska. The notion did not disappear until the Klondike gold rush of 1897–1898, when portions of Alaska seemed rather too valuable to be reserved for criminals. Ted C. Hinckley, "Alaska as an American Botany Bay," *Pacific Historical Review*, XLII (Feb. 1973), 1–19.

56. *Washington National Republican*, Feb. 17, 22, 1869; *Washington Evening Star*, Feb. 24, 25, 1869; *New York Sun*, Feb. 25, 1869.

57. "Alaska Investigation," 1–3.

58. Ibid., 3–4.

59. Ibid., 4–5.

60. Ibid., 6.

61. *Washington Daily Morning Chronicle*, March 4, 1869.

62. *New York Sun, Worcester Daily Spy, Washington Daily Morning Chronicle*, March 1, 1869; *Washington Weekly Chronicle*, March 6, 1869; *Philadelphia Press*, March 1, 1869.

63. *Washington Evening Star*, Feb. 27, 1869. The *Washington National Republican*'s report appeared later and was sketchy, March 1, 1869.

64. *New York Herald*, Feb. 27, 28, 1869.

CH. 4 "THE AFTERMATH OF THE ALASKA SCANDAL"

1. Campbell, *Transformation*, is a recent notable exception to the general thesis that territorial expansionism was unimportant in the late 19th century.

2. Thomas A. Bailey, *A Diplomatic History of the American People* (Englewood Cliffs, N.J.: Prentice-Hall, 9th ed., 1974), 366–71, and Robert H. Ferrell, *American Diplomacy: A History* (New York: Norton, 3d ed., 1975), 282–85, are good-humored examples of how the serious scandals of one generation appear as foibles to another. Ferrell is careful in his evaluation of the crimes.

3. Theodore Clarke Smith, "Expansion after the Civil War, 1865–71," *Political Science Quarterly*, 16 (Sept. 1901), 425; W. Stull Holt, *Treaties Defeated by the Senate: A Study of the Struggle between President and Senate over the Conduct of Foreign Relations* (Baltimore: Johns Hopkins Univ. Press, 1933), 123–29; Jeannette P. Nichols, "The United States Congress and Imperialism, 1861–1897," *Journal of Economic History*, 21 (Dec. 1961), 531; Holbo, "Economics, Emotion, and Expansion," 216–20.

4. John A. Wiltz, *In Search of Peace: The Senate Munitions Inquiry, 1934–36* (Baton Rouge: Louisiana State Univ. Press, 1963); Wayne S. Cole, *Senator Gerald Nye and American Foreign Relations* (Minneapolis: Univ. of Minnesota Press, 1962); Robert A. Divine, *The Reluctant Belligerent* (New York: Wiley, 2nd ed., 1979), 10, 19–38, 67–72.

5. See, for instance, George C. Herring, *America's Longest War: The United States and Vietnam, 1950–1975* (New York: Wiley, 1979), 251, 255, 260; Guenter Lewy, *America in Vietnam* (New York: Oxford Univ. Press, 1978), 222, 415; Robert A. Divine, *Since 1945: Politics and Diplomacy in Recent American History* (2nd ed., New York: Wiley, 1979), 211–15; William C. Westmoreland, *A Soldier Reports* (New York: Dell, 1980), 524, 539. Koreagate, Abscam, and Billygate remain the territory of journalists and jurists. The press has contained countless stories. A particularly worthy article is "The Burden of Billy," *Time*, 116 (Aug. 4, 1980), 12–23.

6. A well-researched study of the background of the affair is Barry Rigby, "Private Interests and the Origins of American Involvement in Samoa, 1872–1877," *The Journal of Pacific History*, VIII (1973), 75–87; Lucius E. Guese, "St. Louis and the Great Whisky Ring," *Missouri Historical Review*, XXXVI (Jan. 1942), 168–83, is a useful analysis. There is no satisfactory account of the fascinating Safe Burglary Cases. Much information appears in the *Washington Evening Star*, Sept. 23 to Oct. 2, 1876, and in other newspapers. A few of the many pieces of evidence connecting Samoa and domestic scandals include *New York Tribune*, *New York Times*,

Washington Evening Star, *New York World*, and *San Francisco Chronicle*, all of April 14, 1876. The Orville Babcock manuscripts in the Newberry Library contain valuable material.

7. *New York Herald*, Feb. 28, 1893, provides ample illustration.

8. Ibid., Feb. 2, 23, 1893; *Washington Evening Star*, Nov. 15, 1893; *Congressional Record*, 53–2, XXVI (Dec. 5, 1893), 29; (Dec. 6, 1893), 65–66.

9. Paul S. Holbo, "The Convergence of Moods and the Cuban-Bond 'Conspiracy' of 1898," *Journal of American History*, LV (June 1968), 54–72.

10. Ibid., 69–72; Lewis L. Gould, *The Presidency of William McKinley* (Lawrence: Regents Press of Kansas, 1980), 98–99, 123–52. The first scandal was in the spring of 1900, ibid., 194–95.

11. *Congressional Globe*, 40–2 (July 1, 1868), 3659–70; *New York Herald*, July 2, 1868.

12. Richardson, ed., *Messages and Papers*, VI, 688–89.

13. *New York Sun*, Feb. 9, 1869.

14. *New York Tribune*, Jan. 14, 1869; *Congressional Globe*, 40–3 (Jan. 13, 1869). For other attacks by the *Tribune* on expansion, see Jan. 9, Feb. 1, 6, 1869.

15. *New York Herald*, Jan. 4, 7, 8, 9, 13, 1868.

16. Ibid., Dec. 10, 1868.

17. Ibid., Dec. 11, 1868.

18. Ibid., Dec. 16, 1868; *San Francisco Alta California*, Dec. 17, 1868. The paper's conjectures were imprecise, since there were two groups of Alta Vela investors, one of which was at odds with the Dominican government.

19. *New York Herald*, Jan. 8, 1869; Charles Callan Tansill, *The United States and Santo Domingo, 1798–1873: A Chapter in Caribbean Diplomacy* (Baltimore: Johns Hopkins Univ. Press, 1938), 216–20, contains some details about the company.

20. *New York Herald*, Jan. 9, 1869.

21. Ibid., Jan. 14, 1869.

22. *Chicago Republican*, Nov. 19, 1870. Sumner was told as early as Dec. 24, 1869, that Fabens and company were involved in a swindle. Tansill, *The United States and Santo Domingo*, 381.

23. *Congressional Globe*, 41–3 (Dec. 9, 1870), 51; (Dec. 12, 1870), 53; (Dec. 20, 1870), 183–97, 217–18; (Dec. 21, 1870), 225–46, 253; Hamilton Fish, Diary, Vol. 2 (Dec. 23, 1870), 147–49; (Jan. 2, 1871), 155; (Jan. 10, 1871), 162; (Jan. 13, 1871), 172; (March 19, 1871), 255; all in Fish Mss., LC; *Washington Daily Patriot*, Dec. 21, 1870, Jan. 9, March 9, 10, 1871; *New York World*, Dec. 29, 1870; Louis A. Coolidge, *Ulysses S. Grant* (Boston: Houghton Mifflin, 1917), 330; Tansill, *The United States and Santo Domingo*, 448; Donald, *Sumner*, 464–97; William Gillette, "Election of 1872," in Arthur M. Schlesinger, Jr., and Fred L. Israel, eds., *History of American Presidential Elections* (New York: Chelsea House, 1971), II, 1306.

24. *New York Herald*, Jan. 21, 24, 26, 27, Feb. 2, 1869.

25. *Washington National Republican*, Feb. 1, 1869.

26. *Washington Daily Morning Chronicle*, Feb. 10, 1869; the *Baltimore Sun*'s report appears in the same edition.

27. *The Nation*, VIII (Feb. 11, 1869), 103.

28. Ibid., "The St. Domingo Bargain," X (Feb. 3, 1870), 68.

29. *New York Herald*, Feb. 27, 28, 1869.

30. *The Nation*, X (Jan. 6, 1870), 5.

31. *New York Herald*, Jan. 12, 1870; see also Jan. 13, 1870.

32. *New York Times*, Jan. 17, 1870. The *Times* had opposed the deal during the Johnson administration; see *New York Times*, Feb. 10, 1869.

33. *New York Tribune*, Jan. 10, 1870; see also Jan. 13, 1870, on the Dominican financial interests of "Judge" Peter O'Sullivan.

34. *The Nation*, "The St. Domingo Bargain," X (Feb. 3, 1870), 68. Godkin seemed most concerned initially about patronage corruption, but his suspicions spread.

35. Tansill, *The United States and Santo Domingo*, 403; Richardson, ed., *Messages and Papers*, VII, 50.

36. Within a week of the Senate's request, J.C.B. Davis of the Department of State warned General Babcock that he had "no hope that the treaty will make its way through the Senate. If there ever was a ghost of a chance the Davis Hatch case will kill it." Davis to Babcock, Feb. 28, 1870, Babcock Mss., Newberry Library. Among the many sources on the Hatch case, see the *New York World*, March 24, 1870, and editions of June 9, 1870, and after in the *World*, *New York Tribune*, *New York Herald*, and other newspapers; *Congressional Globe*, 41-2 (June 8, 1870), 4194ff.; Donald, *Sumner*, 451-52; Sumner Welles, *Naboth's Vineyard* (New York: Payson & Clarke, 1928), 388ff.; Tansill, *The United States and Santo Domingo*, 395-96; E.W. Whitaker to O.E. Babcock, June 9, 1870, Babcock, Mss.; *Executive Journal of the Senate*, June 30, 1870, 500-2; *Select Committee on the Memorial of Davis Hatch*, 41st Congress, 2d Session, Senate, Report No. 234, June 25, 1870, Serial 1409. (This is a 268-page record of testimony, plus majority and minority reports.) See also *Additional Papers in the Case of Davis Hatch, an American Citizen*, 41-2, Senate Misc. Document No. 94, Serial 1408.

37. *Washington Daily Patriot*, Jan. 11, 1871.

38. Roosevelt to Hay, July 22, 1902, vol. 22, Hay Mss., LC.

39. Horace Porter to Nathaniel Banks, Dec. 11, 1870, Box 84, Banks Mss., LC; *Congressional Globe*, 41-3; (Dec. 12, 1870), 53; (Dec. 20, 1870), 183-97; (Dec. 21, 1870), 226-54; (Dec. 22, 1870), 271; (Jan. 9, 1871), 414-16; (Jan. 10, 1871), 408; *Washington Daily Morning Chronicle*, Dec. 21, 22, 23, 1870: *Washington Evening Star*, Dec. 22, 1870, Jan. 14, 1871; *New York Tribune*, Dec. 23, 1870; *Washington Daily Patriot*, Dec. 21, 1870, Jan. 11, 1871; *Autobiography of Andrew Dickson White* (2 vols., New York: Century, 1905), 484-86; Harold Schwartz, *Samuel Gridley Howe, Social Reformer, 1801-1876* (Cambridge: Harvard, 1956), 292-97; Tansill, *The United States and Santo Domingo*, 429-41.

40. Richardson, *Messages*, VII, 128-31. The date was April 5, 1871. Grant's message received considerable attention in the press and Congress and from the public. See, for instance, *New York Herald*, April 6, 8, 10,

1871; *New York Tribune,* April 6, 1871; *New York World,* April 6, 1871; *Washington Evening Star,* April 6, 7, 1871. H.C. Bartlett to Orville Babcock, April 16, 1871, and D.H. Mahan to Orville Babcock, April 17, 1871, are interesting comments. Both these letters are in the Babcock Mss., Newberry Library.

APPENDIX: "WAS BANKS BRIBED?"

1. Dunning, "Paying for Alaska," 385–98.
2. "Alaska Investigation," 11–16.
3. William Archibald Dunning, *Reconstruction, Political and Economic, 1865–1877* (New York: Harper, 1907, 1962), 86–87; "Paying for Alaska," 397.
4. Thomas, *Russo-American Relations,* 160–61.
5. Korngold, *Stevens,* 431–33.
6. Brodie, *Stevens,* 359, 416.
7. Ferrell, *American Diplomacy,* 285.
8. Brodie, *Stevens,* 183–84, with reference to Union Pacific Railroad stocks and bonds, and to Credit Mobilier.
9. Golder, "The Purchase of Alaska," 422–24, implied that Stevens was bought.
10. Welles, *Diary,* II, 469. Banks in succeeding years often expressed his dislike of Sumner in letters to Mrs. Banks; see, for instance, Banks to Mrs. Banks, April 22, 1869, Jan. 8, 1870, Box 3, Banks Mss., LC.
11. Tansill, *The United States and Santo Domingo,* 235–36, 265–66, 275–77; *Congressional Globe,* 40–3 (Jan. 12, 1869), 317–18; Joseph W. Fabens to Banks, Jan. 18, 1869, Box 75, Banks Mss., LC; Seward to Banks, Feb. 5, 1869, Box 76, Banks Mss., LC; Banks to Fabens, Feb. 17, 1869, Fabens Mss., Essex Institute, Salem, Mass.; Banks to Mrs. Banks, March 9, 1869, Box 3, Banks Mss., LC.
12. Dunning, "Paying for Alaska," 397.
13. See, for example, Miller, "The Alaska Treaty," 532–44; Thomas, *Russo-American Relations,* 162, qualified on 160. Tansill, *The United States and Santo Domingo,* 356, footnote 41, sharply criticized Banks over the affair and accused him of favoring imperialism "to line his pockets."
14. Harrington, *Fighting General,* 184, 197.
15. Ibid., 262, footnote 89, and 197.
16. Ibid., 197, 263, footnote 3.
17. Ibid., 262, footnote 88; Banks to Mary Banks and to "Dearest Mother," Jan. 15, 1863, Box 3, Banks Mss., LC.
18. Harrington, *Fighting General,* 262, footnote 90; Banks to Mrs. Banks, Sept. 7, 1865, Nov. 22, 1867, Box 3, Banks Mss., LC.
19. Banks Diary, 1867, Box 1, Banks Mss., LC.
20. Ibid., 1868.
21. Banks to Mrs. Banks, March 9, May 3, 1869, Box 3, Banks Mss., LC.

22. Mrs. Banks to Banks, Jan. 8, 1870, Box 2, Banks Mss., LC.

23. Mrs. Banks to Banks, Feb. 9, 1871, Box 2, Banks Mss., LC.

24. Mrs. Banks to Banks, May 21, 1871, Box 2, Banks, Mss., LC.

25. Statement, Oct. 16, 1869, Box 79, Banks Mss., LC.

26. Banks to Mrs. Banks, June 20, 22, 1869, Box 3, Banks Mss., LC.

27. James L. Anders (clerk) to Banks, Oct. 5, 1869, Box 79, Banks Mss., LC.

28. C.C. Andrews to Carl Ehmann (U.S. Legation, Stockholm), Sept. 30, 1869, Box 79, Banks Mss., LC; Nathan Appleton to Banks, Jan. 14, 1870, C.B. Norton to Banks, Jan. 14, 21, Feb. 18, 1870; Banks to Appleton, Jan. 31, 1870, Box 80, Banks Mss., LC.

29. Banks to Mrs. Banks, Oct. 1869, Box 3, Banks Mss., LC.

30. Banks to Mrs. Banks, Oct. 28, 1869, Box 3, Banks Mss., LC.

31. Banks to Mrs. Banks, Oct. 1869, Box 3, Banks Mss., LC.

32. Banks to Mrs. Banks, Jan. 12, 1870, Box 3, Banks Mss., LC.

33. Banks Diary, 1873, Box 1, Banks Mss., LC.

AN ESSAY ON THE LITERATURE

The primary reference for literature on American foreign relations after 1865, including an analysis of the major historical issues, is "Expansion Following the Civil War, 1865–1898," a chapter compiled and edited by Paul S. Holbo for the *Guide to U.S. Foreign Relations Since 1700* (Santa Barbara: ABC-Clio, 1983). The *Guide*, a massive annotated reference work with 9,000 entries, was prepared for publication by general editor Richard Dean Burns and was sponsored by the Society for Historians of American Foreign Relations. Where the authoritative *Guide* is not available, students may be able to consult the excellent bibliographical essay by Charles S. Campbell, in his major work, *The Transformation of American Foreign Relations, 1865–1900* (New York: Harper, 1976).

Perceptive appraisals of the extensive arguments about late nineteenth-century foreign policy are to be found in David Healy, *Modern Imperialism: Changing Styles in Historical Interpretation* (Washington, D.C.: American Historical Association, 1967); Ernest R. May, *American Imperialism: A Speculative Essay* (New York: Atheneum, 1968); and Robert L. Beisner, *From the Old Diplomacy to the New, 1865–1900* (New York: Crowell, 1964). Annotations covering many books and articles follow each chapter in Thomas A. Bailey, *A Diplomatic History of the American People* (10th ed., New York: Prentice-Hall, 1980). The bibliographies in some other textbooks in diplomatic history are also helpful. Of use, as well, are two bibliographic compilations: Norman A. Graebner, *American Diplomatic History Before 1900* (Arlington Heights, Ill.: AHM, 1978), and Vincent P. De Santis, *The Gilded Age, 1877–1896* (Arlington Heights, Ill.: AHM, 1973), which covers politics in addition to foreign relations.

The best guide to material on the purchase of Alaska is the thoughtful commentary prepared by Ronald J. Jensen for the chapter, "Expansion Following the Civil War," mentioned above. Jensen's book, *The Alaska Purchase and Russian-American Relations* (Seattle: Univ. of Washington Press, 1975), also contains annotated bibliographical references. Useful citations are to be found in Howard I. Kushner, *Conflict on the Northwest Coast: American-Russian Rivalry in the Pacific Northwest, 1790–1867* (Westport, Conn.: Greenwood, 1975).

Before discussing some of the important books and articles treated in the above bibliographies, it is necessary to comment upon several essential primary sources. Russian materials are not readily available, but there is a small collection of documents pertaining to Russian America in the Manuscripts Division of the Library of Congress. These items, which are listed as I-9, No. 4, and total 125 pages, include translated letters and committee reports. One piece, a long letter from Stoeckl to Gorchakov in 1859/1860, has been printed in the *Pacific Historical Review*, III (1934), 80–87.

A vast amount of documentary material exists on the United States side. Readily available in research libraries is the compilation prepared by the Department of State in response to the request for information by the House of Representatives on December 19, 1867. Seward responded on February 17, 1868, with the carefully selected collection printed as U.S. House, 40th Congress, 2d Session, Volume 13, Executive Document No. 177, Series 1339. It includes the petition of Washington Territory in 1866, an 1864 letter from Seward to Cassius Clay, a copy of the treaty of cession (in French and English), much of Seward's correspondence with Stoeckl (largely after the cession), several dozen letters to Seward from Americans and journalistic pieces favoring the treaty, Russian surveys and American maps of Alaska, and (for over 200 pages) Sumner's interminable "speech."

Another key documentary source is Report No. 35, entitled "Alaska Investigation," of the Committee on Public Expenditures of the House of Representatives, 40th Congress, 3d Session. This report — like Seward's compilation mentioned above — is incomplete, but it is valuable nevertheless, especially if supplemented by use of newspaper reports. Finally, the *Congressional Globe* must be mentioned, because its coverage of congressional debates and action is of great utility for understanding Alaska and related subjects such as Johnson's policies, impeachment, scandals, and government finances.

Not a document as such but in a category by itself is the lengthy manuscript, "The Alaska Treaty," prepared by David Hunter Miller, a lawyer who helped to draft the Covenant of the League of Nations and who later, as Historical Advisor to the Department of State, became the historian of a number of important American treaties. His comprehensive, highly detailed analysis covers the subject from the Russian administration of the territory through the settlement of the Perkins claim. The manuscript, which was completed during the Second World War and would have been volume nine in the official series, was never published. It is available for use, howver, in microform (Microcopy No. T-1024, Drawer 10-19-1) at the National Archives. All serious students of the subject must consult it.

The single best book on its subject is *The Alaska Purchase and Russian-American Relations*, by Richard Jensen, referred to earlier. Jensen carefully analyzed the negotiations from 1854 through 1868. In the author's view, strategic motives were determining elements for both governments. Victor John Farrar, *The Annexation of Russian America to the United States* (Washington, D.C.: W.F. Roberts, 1937), contains useful material but is inaccurate in important details and outdated in interpretation. A brief summary of some of the more significant recent views appears in John L. Gaddis, *Russia, the Soviet Union and the United States: An Interpretive History* (New York: Wiley, 1978).

The so-called New Left or revisionist historians comprise a distinct school of thought on the acquisition of Alaska. These writers believe that American economic expansion and competition with Russia determined events. The most important works in this vein include: William Appleman Williams, *American-Russian Relations, 1781–1947* (New York: Rinehart, 1952), which is the seminal volume; Walter La Feber, *The New Empire: An Interpretation of American Expansion, 1860–1898* (Ithaca: Cornell Univ. Press, 1963), which stressed Seward's interest in Alaska as a bridge to Asian markets; Charles Vevier, "The Collins Overland Line and American Continentalism," *Pacific Historical Review*, 27 (1959), 237–53, which contended that the unsuccessful effort of an American promoter to organize a telegraph line to Russia through Russian America made the territory seem an important commercial link; Ernest N. Paolino, *The Foundations of American Empire: William Henry Seward and U.S. Foreign Policy* (Ithaca: Cornell Univ. Press, 1973), which held that the secretary had a systematic view of foreign policy, with commerce playing the leading part; and a book mentioned earlier, Howard I. Kushner, *Conflict on the Northwest Coast*, in which it was argued that American expansion of fishing, whaling, and commerce led to conflict and that Russia ceded the territory to avoid its seizure by the United States.

A broader view appears in the volume edited by Morgan B. Sherwood, *Alaska and Its History* (Seattle: Univ. of Washington Press, 1967), which consists of articles assessing events from the Russian occupation through American settlement. Also sweeping in scope is the pioneer study by Hubert H. Bancroft, *History of Alaska, 1730–1885* (San Francisco: A.L. Bancroft, 1886). Bancroft stressed the colonial period; in discussing the cession, he emphasized Russian fears of a British takeover.

A number of works have dealt at greater length with the period of Russian control and with Russian motives for the cession. A good introduction is Hector Chevigny, *Russian-American, 1741–1867* (New York: Viking, 1965), which deals particularly with exploration of the territory and the development of the Russian-American Company. S.B. Okun employed Russian materials for his treatment of the company's financial problems, in *The Russian-American Company* (Cambridge: Harvard Univ. Press, 1951). In an earlier study, "The Purchase of Alaska," *American Historical Review*, 25 (April 1920), 411–25, Frank Golder contended that Russia was eager to be rid of a burden and that Seward's motivation was political; the Russian sources quoted by Golder remain of great value for evaluating the negotiations and the issue of Russian financial payments. Benjamin Thomas, *Russo-American Relations, 1815–1867* (Baltimore: Johns Hopkins Univ. Press, 1930), emphasized, as did Okun, the decline of the Russian-American Company as the key to the cession. Anatole G. Mazour used some Russian sources not available to Golder in his article, "The Prelude to Russia's Departure from America," *Pacific Historical Review* 10 (1941), 311–19, and described distractions for Russia in Asia but emphasized Russia's difficulty in holding her American territory and her desire for a blow at England. David Hunter Miller, "Russian Opinion on the Cession of Alaska," *American Historical Review*, 48 (1943), 521–31, reproduced an 1866 Russian document urging retention of the territory. Those interested in studying other documents on the Russian side should consult Frank A. Golder, *Guide to Materials for American*

History in Russian Archives, 2 vols. (Washington, D.C.: Carnegie Institution, 1917–1937).

Biographies and memoirs are among the most available sources of information on the purchase and its aftermath. Hallie M. McPherson, "The Interest of William McKendree Gwin in the Purchase of Alaska, 1854–1861," *Pacific Historical Review*, 3 (1934), 28–38, remains the best study of that precursor of expansion to Alaska. *Memoirs of Cornelius Cole: Ex-Senator of the United States from California* (New York: McLoughlin, 1908), includes some relevant information about another West Coast expansionist. H. Edward Richardson developed a sharp portrait of his flamboyant subject in *Cassius Marcellus Clay: Firebrand of Freedom* (Lexington: Univ. of Kentucky Press, 1976). James P. Shenton, *Robert John Walker: A Politician from Jackson to Lincoln* (New York: Columbia Univ. Press, 1961), is the best biography of that tireless expansionist, but Shenton failed to probe some important issues. An older essay is William E. Dodd, *Robert J. Walker, Imperialist* (Chicago: Literary Club, 1914, rpt. Gloucester: Peter Smith, 1967).

The major figure in the acquisition of Alaska is the subject of an impressive biography by G.G. Van Deusen, *William Henry Seward* (New York: Oxford Univ. Press, 1967), which stressed the secretary's expansionist vision and strategic concerns. It should be supplemented by Gordon H. Warren's probing essay, "Imperial Dreamer: William Henry Seward and American Destiny," in Frank Merli and Theodore Wilson, editors, *Makers of American Diplomacy* (New York: Scribner's, 1974), I, 195–221; Frederick Seward, editor, *Seward at Washington as Senator and Secretary of State: A Memoir of his Life with Sections from His Letters, 1861–1872*, 3 vols., (New York: Derby and Miller, 1891); and Frederick Bancroft, *The Life of William H. Seward*, 2 vols., (New York: Harper, 1900). There are a number of biographies of Andrew Johnson, but none provides much information about the Alaska purchase. Among the readily available books is Lately Thomas, *The First President Johnson: The Three Lives of the Seventeenth President of the United States of America* (New York: Morrow, 1968). *The Trial of Andrew Johnson* (Washington, D.C.: GPO, 1868), the key documentary source, contains valuable contextual material. *Diary of Gideon Welles: Secretary of the Navy Under Lincoln and Johnson*, ed. Howard K. Beale and Allen Brownsword, 3 vols. (New York: Norton, 1960), provides some insights about a cabinet opponent of expansion.

As for members of Congress involved in the purchase, David H. Donald, *Charles Sumner and the Rights of Man* (New York: Knopf, 1970), is comprehensive and penetrating. Sumner's own view appears in his *Memoirs and Letters of Charles Sumner*, 4 vols. (Boston: Lee and Shepard, 1877–93), the fourth volume of which includes the issue of cession and the Alaska speech. Edward L. Pierce, *Memoir and Letters of Charles Sumner (London: Sampson, Low, Marston*, 1893), is perhaps the best of the several Sumnerphilic biographies. Fawn Brodie, *Thaddeus Stevens: Scourge of the South* (New York: Norton, 1959, 1966), is the most useful of several books; for comparison, examine Ralph Korngold, *Thaddeus Stevens: A Being Darkly Wise and Rudely Great* (New York: Harcourt, Brace, 1955). Ben Butler deserves a new study that would explore the paradoxes in his later political career. The best existing work is Hans L. Trefousse, *Ben Butler: The South Called Him Beast* (New York: Twayne, 1957); see also Robert S. Holzman, *Stormy Ben Butler* (New York: Macmillan, 1934). Fred Harvey Harrington, *Fighting Politician: Major General N.P. Banks* (Philadelphia: Univ. of Pennsylvania Press, 1948), capably described his subject's ardent expansionism, but the book's documentation and treatment of Banks's financial interests are unreliable.

Among other biographical works that should be consulted are the following: John Bigelow, ed., *Tilden's Letters and Literary Memorials* (New York: Harper, 1980), which contains much revealing material; Bigelow, *Retrospections of an Active Life, 1867–1871* (New York: Doubleday, 1913), includes the distinguished editor's questionable recollection of his conversation with Seward about Russian payoffs; Alexander C. Flick, *Samuel Jones Tilden: A Study in Political Sagacity* (New York: Dodd, Mead, 1939), rich in political detail; G.G. Van Deusen, *Thurlow Weed: Wizard of the Lobby* (Boston: Little, Brown, 1947), thin on the late 1860s; Claude Fuess, *The Life of Caleb Cushing*, 2 vols. (New York: Harcourt, Brace, 1923; Hamden, Archon, 1965); Henry Cohen, *Business and Politics in America from the Age of Jackson to the Civil War: The Career Biography of W.W. Corcoran* (Westport, Conn.: Greenwood, 1971); W.W. Corcoran, *A Grandfather's Legacy; Containing a Sketch of His Life . . . Together with Letters from His Friends* (Washington, D.C.: Henry Polkinhorne, 1879), which contains letters from Walker to Corcoran; Irving Katz, *August Belmont: A Political Biography* (New York: Columbia Univ. Press, 1968), which suffers from minor errors; Stewart Mitchell, *Horatio Seymour of New York* (Cambridge: Harvard Univ. Press, 1938). Political studies of considerable value include: George Fort Milton, *The Age of Hate: Andrew Johnson and the Radicals* (New York: Coward-McCann, 1930); Charles H. Coleman, *The Election of 1868: The Democratic Effort to Regain Control* (New York: Columbia Univ. Press, 1933); and Roy F. Nichols, *The Disruption of American Democracy* (New York: Macmillan, 1948).

There are three fine studies of editorial opinion on the acquisition of Alaska: Thomas A. Bailey, "Why the United States Purchased Alaska," *Pacific Historical Review* 3 (1934), 39–49; Virginia Hancock Reid, *The Purchase of Alaska: Contemporary Opinion* (Long Beach: Press-Telegram, 1940); Richard E. Welch, "American Public Opinion and the Purchase of Russian America," *American Slavic and East European Review*, 17 (1958), 481–94.

Two early studies of the Alaska scandal that must be read are William A. Dunning, "Paying for Alaska," *Political Science Quarterly*, 27 (1912), 385–98, which featured Johnson's now-famed memorandum written after his picnic with Seward; and Reinhard Luthin, "The Sale of Alaska," *Slavonic and East European Review*, 16 (1937), 168–82. See also the works by Farrar, Miller, and Jensen. Excellent sources for a broader understanding of political corruption in the United States are Arthur M. Schlesinger, Jr., and Roger Bruns, eds., *Congress Investigates: A Documentary History, 1792–1974*, 5 vols. (New York: Chelsea, 1975); Morton Keller, *Affairs of State: Public Life in Late Nineteenth Century America* (Cambridge: Harvard Univ. Press, 1977); and Abraham S. Eisenstadt, Ari Hoogenboom, and Hans L. Trefousse, eds., *Before Watergate: Problems of Corruption in American Society* (New York: Columbia Univ. Press, 1979). A helpful and entertaining monograph is Alexander B. Callow, Jr., *The Tweed Ring* (New York: Oxford Univ. Press, 1965).

Expansionist issues concurrent with the purchase of Alaska are treated fully if not always dispassionately in Charles C. Tansill, *The Purchase of the Danish West Indies* (Baltimore: Johns Hopkins Univ. Press, 1932), and *The United States and Santo Domingo, 1789–1873* (Baltimore: Johns Hopkins Univ. Press, 1938). See also Brainerd Dyer, "Robert J. Walker on Acquiring Greenland and Iceland," *Mississippi Valley Historical Review*, 27 (1940), 263–66.

Those interested in the initial image and the subsequent development of Alaska following the purchase should consult two fine works by Ted C. Hinckley: "Alaska as an American Botany Bay," *Pacific Historical Review*, 42 (1973), 1–19, and *The Americanization of Alaska, 1867–1897* (Palo Alto: Pacific Books, 1972), which carries the story to the gold rush. The notes to these works will serve as guides for still further reading.

The notes of the fourth chapter contain many references to relations with the Dominican Republic, Samoa, and Hawaii. A more comprehensive bibliographical listing on these subjects and on the late nineteenth century in general has become available with the publication of the *Guide*. Barry Rigby, "American Expansion in Hawaii: The Contribution of Henry A. Peirce," *Diplomatic History*, 4 (Fall 1980), 353–69, and David M. Pletcher, "Rhetoric and Results: A Pragmatic View of American Economic Expansionism, 1865–1896," *Diplomatic History*, 5 (Spring 1981), 93–105, are recent valuable articles. Thomas J. Osborne, *"Empire Can Wait": American Opposition to Hawaiian Annexation, 1893–1898*, (Kent, Ohio: Kent State Univ. Press, 1981), analyzes effectively the actions of the Cleveland administration on Hawaiian annexation and the development of an opposition to expansion in the 1890s. Interesting details about the response of the McKinley administration to Japanese actions regarding Hawaii appear in William Michael Morgan, "The Anti-Japanese Origins of the Hawaiian Annexation Treaty of 1897," *Diplomatic History*, 6 (Winter 1982), 23–44. A comprehensive and detailed analysis of the foreign policy of the McKinley administration is included in Lewis L. Gould, *The Presidency of William McKinley* (Lawrence: Regents Press of Kansas, 1980).

INDEX

Tarnished Expansion has been composed on a Compugraphic digital phototypesetter in ten point Caledonia with two points of spacing between the lines. Roman and Italic Bulmer was selected for display. The book was designed by Jim Billingsley, set into type by Metricomp, Inc., printed offset by Thomson-Shore, Inc., and bound by John H. Dekker & Sons. The paper on which the book is printed bears the watermark of S. D. Warren and is designed for an effective life of at least three hundred years.

THE UNIVERSITY OF TENNESSEE PRESS : KNOXVILLE

TARNISHED EXPANSION

The Alaska Scandal, the Press, and Congress, 1867–1871

Paul S. Holbo

In this book, Paul S. Holbo develops an arresting new thesis about the pattern of American foreign relations in the late nineteenth century and about American politics generally. By describing the revelations in the press and analyzing the scandal and investigation that followed the congressional appropriation for the purchase of Alaska, he demonstrates that real and alleged corruption affected American foreign policy during the Gilded Age, as in later times.

It is the author's view that an idealistic territorial expansionism was very much alive in the United States following the Civil War but that nothing resulted from it between 1867 and 1898 because recurring scandals, beginning with the Alaska affair, eroded political and popular support for expansionist policies. After studying the Alaska scandal in detail, Holbo argues that memories of this controversy stymied the Caribbean ambitions of President Ulysses S. Grant and tarnished later expansionist ventures in the Pacific. His